Rag Rug

HANDBOOK

Janet Meany & Paula Pfaff

Illustrations by Suzanne Baizerman

INTERWEAVE PRESS

This book is dedicated with deep affection and
appreciation to rag rug weavers everywhere,
and to the next generation of weavers in the hope that
they, too, will pass this unique heritage along
to their sons and daughters.

Editors: Karen Searle, Susan Larson-Fleming
Illustrations: Suzanne Baizerman
Interior Design: Patrick Redmond
Cover Design: Keith Rosenhagen, Graphic Relations
Production: Marc McCoy Owens
Black-and-White Photography: Suzanne Baizerman, Karen Searle
Photo of Janet Meany: Bruce Ojard
Photo of Paula Pfaff: Nancy Goodman

Cover Fabric: woven and designed by Paula Pfaff; photographed by Peter Lee

The Newcomb Loom Co. images courtesy of The Newcomb Looms Historical
Society; other historical illustrations loaned from private collections

Text copyright © 1996 Janet Meany and Paula Pfaff

Interweave Press, Inc.
201 East Fourth Street
Loveland, Colorado 80537 USA
www.interweave.com

Library of Congress Cataloging-in-Publication Data

Meany, Janet
    Rag rug handbook / Janet Meany & Paula Pfaff ; illustrations by
Suzanne Baizerman.
        p.   cm.
    Includes bibliographical references and index.
    ISBN 1-883010-28-4
    1. Rag rugs. 2. Hand weaving. I. Pfaff, Paula. II. Title.
TT850.M44 1996
746.7'2—dc20   96-9504
                                                                    CIP

Originally published 1988 by Dos Tejedoras Fiber Arts Publications

10 9 8 7 6

Table of Contents

Acknowledgments

Our thanks to Dos Tejedoras Fiber Arts Publications and its editors for first publishing this book, and Interweave Press and its editors for reprinting it.

To the rag rug weavers of Minnesota for opening their homes and sharing their skills and affection for weaving.

To all those who have told us about their techniques, their patterns and their plans for "the next rug".

To the students of the beginning and intermediate Rag Rug classes at the Weaver's Guild of Minnesota, the Fiber Handcrafters Guild, and the Split Rock Arts Program for their encouragement, interest, and enthusiasm.

To the following persons who have contributed in important ways: Rora Strom, Julie Widen, Irene Ronning, Helga Johnson, Myrtle Penner, James Russell Deen, Georgia Knierem, Frank Knierem, Terry Poffenbarger, Virginia Voss, Wanda Lynn of The Oriental Rug Company, the Adair family of the Edgemont Yarn Service, Irja Wattunen, Susan Saari-Karasti, Carol Sperling, Lila Nelson of Vesterheim, The Norwegian-American Museum, Gene E. Valk, Linda Madden, Donna Sovick, Ruby Jansen, Theresa Lee Trebon of The Newcomb Looms Historical Society, Sister Geraldine Biron, Mary Cook, Mildred Carselle, Susan Barker, Carl and Edna Elsaser, Ina Karni, Esther Kyromaki, Susan Gustafson, Heather Reed, Margaret Sande, Leo Perry, Johanna Erickson, Penny Casler, Missy Stevens, Mary Anne Wise, Nancy Potek, Marge Polanek, and Phyllis Waggoner.

Opposite. Trade post card from the Newcomb Loom Company, ca. 1890. An advertisement for the "Weaver's Friend" hand loom appears on the back. *Collection of Janet Meany.*

A Tradition Continues

To create a rug with a pattern design to match the beauty of a summer sunset, even to match a fussy customer's kitchen color scheme, is as much an art as painting a scene on canvas. . . . Something of the wonder of it is what a skilled weaver with a mite of imagination can make from old, worn-out men's overalls, socks, nylons, bed blankets, spreads, ginghams, and whatnots. Even old tapestry upholstering [sic] from a couch or love seat can be given a butterfly's splendorous rebirth as a rug.

Mrs. Marietta Schram
The Shuttle, Spring 1964

Loom that belonged to the late Katri Saari, Angora, Minnesota. The curved central rear support is constructed from a single piece of wood. *Photo by Ken Moran.*

We are avid rug weavers and teachers of weaving who enjoy helping people get started in the historic craft of rag rug weaving. Paula relates the following incident, which is typical of our experiences.

Several years ago, I received a call from Mary Cook. She said, "I want to learn how to weave rag rugs. Will you teach me? I'm 78 years old, so I'll have to do it now!"

Not fully expecting her to follow through, I suggested she take the beginning floor loom class at our area weavers guild. Once she mastered the basics, I would teach her to weave rugs. Six months later, my phone rang again. It was Mary. "Well, I've taken the floor loom class and bought a loom. *Now* can we begin?"

Mary suggested spending a day with me watching what I do. She arrived armed with two kinds of cookies, a loaf of homemade bread, and strawberry jam. We discovered that we had much in common, as many weavers do. We had a wonderful time together that day and many more after that. A determined student, Mary learned to warp the loom with some help from her husband and became a rag rug weaver. She developed her own trademark of laying in short accent strips on top of the rags. She made rugs for all of her grandchildren as well as for her church fund-raisers.

Rag rugs are part of a continuing legacy handed on from one generation to the next. Once common in almost every home, rag rugs were found at the back door, in front of the kitchen sink, and beside the bed. Discarded family clothing was recycled—wound into balls of rag strips and taken to the local weaver to be woven into rugs. Old rugs often contained the family history and provided opportunities for reminiscing about the past. Scraps of Mother's house dresses and aprons, Dad's work shirts, flour sacks, and bed covers, even Grandma's bloomers ended up on the floor!

Our objective has been to gather information on rag weaving techniques, patterns, and old rug looms. Certain favorite patterns have been handed down from weaver to weaver for decades. We found many patterns in old loom instruction books or by studying old rugs. Some were learned during visits with fellow weavers, with whom we spent delightful afternoons hearing memories of the past. It is our hope that in recording these patterns and techniques, the rag rug tradition will continue.

This book is meant to serve as a handbook for weaving rag rugs. *Chapter One* gives instructions for weaving a first rug: equipment, warp calculation, rag preparation, weaving, and finishing. *Chapter Two* contains further information on warp yarns, other techniques of rag preparation, and valuable hints for selvedges, headings, and finishings. We have recorded several methods, stressing those we prefer. We also include a variety of suggestions and hints gleaned from old books and from experienced weavers.

In *Chapter Three*, we discuss many common rag rug weaves and their variations. For those looking for specific projects with detailed directions, the projects in *Chapter Four* cover both basic two-shaft and four-shaft weaves.

Chapter Five outlines a general history of rag rugs. In this chapter, we have also tried to identify a number of looms, both handmade and factory-built, that have been used for rag rug weaving. Because resource material on this subject is scarce, we have listed manufacturers and suppliers wherever possible. The *Appendix* contains several approaches to warping. An extensive *Bibliography* includes references to books helpful for many types of looms. The *Suppliers List* contains ordering information for basic rag weaving supplies and reprints of old rug loom manuals.

It is in the spirit of sharing that we present this book. We have attempted to meet the needs of the beginning rag rug weaver as well as to provide inspiration for years of satisfying and productive weaving.

Chapter One

Getting Started: Weaving a First Rug

M̲y children all say I never buy anything without first deciding if it will look nice in a rug after it's worn out. I'm afraid this is almost true. I always check bedspreads for fast colors because they make such lovely soft rugs.

Ruth D. Stock
The Shuttle, Fall 1964

Counterbalanced Loom
"Sinking Shed"
1. Roller with cords
2. Shafts
3. Heddles
4. Back Beam
5. Warp Beam
6. Crank for warp beam
7. Ratchets
8. Tie-up Cords
9. Treadles
10. Brake Release Lever
11. Cloth Beam
12. Lever for front ratchet
13. Breast Beam
14. Beater
15. Reed
16. Shuttle Race
17. Shuttle

Jack Loom
"Rising Shed"
1. Castle
2. Shafts
3. Beater
4. Reed
5. Shuttle Race
6. Cloth Beam
7. Apron
8. Lever for front ratchet
9. Breast Beam
10. Brake Release Lever
11. Lamms
12. Treadles
13. Tie-up Cords
14. Sectional Warp Beam
15. Back Beam

Directions are given here for weaving a back door/kitchen sink rug. This type of rug is usually woven of cotton carpet warp and cotton rags. The length is 36 to 40 inches and the standard width is 28 inches, allowing the rug to fit through a doorway comfortably and making it easy to shake and wash.

Loom

A sturdy loom is essential for a tightly-woven rag rug. Many looms are available, both new and used, that are suitable for weaving rag rugs. Old handmade looms can weave very well if you are willing to take the time to adjust shafts and, possibly, to reconstruct parts. Factory-built rag rug looms can be purchased used or new. Used looms may be found at garage sales, estate sales, or through classified ads. Weaving magazines can provide information on loom companies.

A two- or four-shaft loom is suitable for rag rug weaving. See illustration, page 5. The loom should have a heavy *beater*. The rags need to be "beat" into place to form a firm fabric. Extra weight can be added by attaching a metal rod to the beater. See figure 1-1. Weaving rugs is heavy physical work, so the heavier the loom and beater, the more efficient the weaving.

The action of the beater during weaving causes the loom to "walk" or to move toward the weaver. Most looms need to be placed either on carpet, pads of foam rubber, or fixed in place on the floor with bolts or braces from the wall. See figure 1-2.

A useful feature to have on your loom is a *cloth beam* with a large storage capacity so that a number of rugs can be woven before cutting them off and starting again. Many looms have sectional back beams (with pegs every one or two inches) that can accommodate very long warps, up to 100 yards or more.

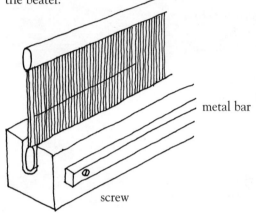

1-1. **Adding weight to the beater.** Attach an iron bar to the lower back portion of the beater.

metal bar

screw

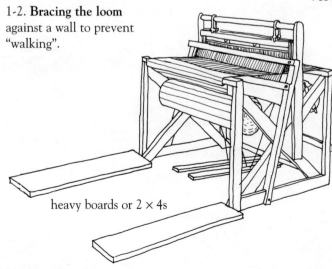

1-2. **Bracing the loom** against a wall to prevent "walking".

heavy boards or 2 × 4s

Shuttles

Several types of shuttles are suitable for carrying rag wefts. See figure 1-3. The *classic rag shuttle* is a rather large and bulky tool 18 to 20 inches long and 3 inches deep with the braces 14 inches apart. Since most rag rugs are 28 inches wide, one wrap around the shuttle is equal to one "shot" of weft across the rug, making the counting of weft shots and pattern rows easier. These shuttles often come with old looms or they can be purchased new.

Another shuttle that is equally popular is the *ski shuttle*. The smooth, flat bottom helps even very thick rags slide through the warp easily.

Stick shuttles—smooth, flat sticks that are notched at both ends—may also be used for rags. Winding the rag in a figure-eight motion on each side allows more rags to be put on the shuttle. See figure 1-3D. The figure-eight winding method also makes the shuttle flatter for easier weaving.

It is best to have many shuttles (6 to 10) so that all the rags for an entire rug can be cut and wound on the shuttles before starting to weave. The shuttles can then be laid out in order and the weaving done in an uninterrupted manner.

Warp

Because rag rugs need to be tight and firm, you need a strong warp yarn that resists abrasion. The most commonly used warp is *8/4 cotton carpet warp*. It is inexpensive, available in many colors, and wears quite well. Cotton carpet warp can be purchased by mail order or from yarn and craft shops. One 8-ounce tube contains 800 yards of warp. Each individual warp thread is called an *end*.

To determine the number of warp ends per inch needed for the loom, count the number of slots in a one-inch section of the reed. This determines the number of *ends per inch*, or *e.p.i.*, usually 10 or 12.

One rug 4½ feet long requires 3 yards of warp on the loom. The weaving process "takes up" warp as the warp travels over and under the rags. Twenty percent of the desired rug length is added for take-up. Fringe allowance of 6 to 12 inches at each end and loom waste of one yard for most looms account for the rest of the warp length.

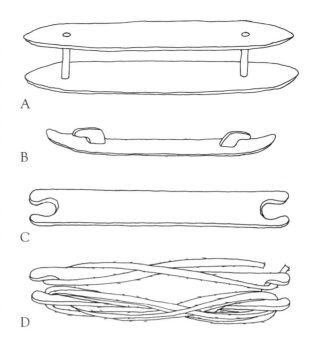

A

B

C

D

1-3. **Shuttles** suitable for carrying rags. A) Rag shuttle. B) Ski shuttle. C) Stick shuttle. D) Winding rags in a figure-eight onto stick shuttle.

The *warp length* for one rug is calculated as follows:

Finished rug length (inches) + 20% take-up + 12" fringe + 36" loom waste = warp length.

Divide by 36 to find warp length in yards.

The *number of warp ends* for one rug is calculated as follows:

12 e.p.i. × 28" = 336 ends. 336 ends × 3 yards = 1008 yards of warp.

Because there are 800 yards per tube, two tubes of warp in the same color are needed.

The color of the warp may either contrast or blend with the rag filler, depending on your preference. Unwind some warp and lay it out over the rags to get an idea of what it will look like when woven. It is always a surprise to see the rags actually woven and even more exciting to see the rug on the floor where the colors blend together or form distinct designs.

The next step is to warp the loom. At first, this is a slow and often frustrating part of weaving. However, most weavers agree that it becomes more pleasant and certainly easier as the weaver gains experience and confidence. See *Appendix One* for a basic warping method.

After the loom is threaded, the shafts need to be tied to the treadles (the *tie-up*) to produce the two plain-weave sheds. If your loom has only two shafts, attach one shaft to each treadle. If you have a four-shaft loom, attach shafts 1 and 3 to one treadle and shafts 2 and 4 to another. More information on tie-ups appears in *Chapter Four*.

Rag Weft

The term *rags* refers to any fabric, new or old, that is cut into strips and woven. The type of rag used determines the color, texture, thickness, and durability of the rug. All fabrics can be utilized: cottons, cotton blends, knits (all kinds), synthetics, and wool. Often used, for example, are old chenille bedspreads, blankets, sheets, table linens, clothing, blue jeans, coats, suits—even neckties and old pantyhose and tights. Towels can be recycled into great rag rug bath mats.

In general, different types of material should not be mixed within the same rug. Use all-wool or all-cotton, but not both in the same rug. Most fabrics should be preshrunk, if possible, to minimize shrinkage of the finished rug and to soften the fabric for easier weaving.

Sources for old rags are endless and there is no shortage of inexpensive or free materials. Asking friends and relatives or church groups for rags will usually bring in a lifetime supply. Garage and rummage sales are also good sources.

How Much Fabric Do I Need?

There are no definite answers, merely guidelines. Many factors will enter into your calculations, such as weight of the fabric, size of the rug, width of the strip, and individual weaving style.

Use a scale, such as a baby scale or a kitchen scale, to weigh fabrics before weaving. Subtract the weight of leftovers and keep a record of the amount used, the type of fabric, rug length, and warp sett. Follow this practice and you will develop guidelines suitable for your weaving.

Start with five pounds of fabric for your first rug.

Basic Rug Weaving

Rag rug weaving is much like weaving with yarn. The main differences are that the warp tension needs to be kept very tight and the rags must be beaten very firmly in place.

Filler

These first "shots" of rag or yarn will prevent the rug from raveling when cut off the loom and will also spread the warp, starting you off with an even selvedge. Do not use smooth, slippery yarns or rags for this spreading filler. See figure 1-4.

1. *Wind a shuttle* with some old rag strips or scrap yarns.

2. *Treadle the first shed.* This will raise every other warp end. Insert the shuttle and lay the rag diagonally across the web, 6 to 8 inches above the fell line. This will allow enough slack for the rag to go over and under the warps without drawing them in at the edges.

3. *Beat hard, then change the shed.* The opposite set of warp ends will be raised. Beat once again, sharp and hard. Insert the shuttle from the other side, angling the rag as before. Beat as you close the shed, then beat again.

I will say the best rule I have found for dividing rags is to weigh each color separately and reduce the weight to ounces then multiply by 12 (allowing 12 shots to an ounce of rags), then divide by the number of yards I want to make; that will give the number of shots that color will make in a yard; then divide by the number of stripes wanted in a yard. The above rule is for cotton or light worsted rags.

Mrs. M. A. Stevenson
The Weaver's Herald, April 1894

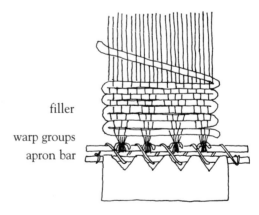

filler

warp groups

apron bar

1-4. **Filler** of yarn or rags woven in to spread warp.

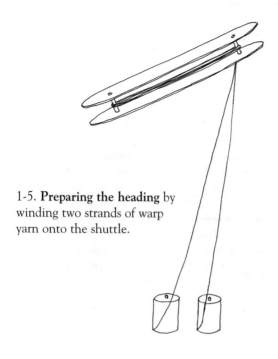

1-5. **Preparing the heading** by winding two strands of warp yarn onto the shuttle.

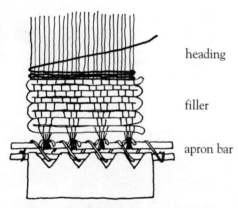

heading

filler

apron bar

1-6. **Weaving the heading** with doubled warp yarn for border or hem.

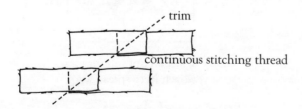

trim

continuous stitching thread

1-7. **Joining a series of rag strips** by machine. Overlap two ends and stitch diagonally across the join. Do not cut stitching thread between rag joins until ready to use. Trim off "ears".

Continue filling until the warp is evenly spread. Now is the time to check for possible threading errors and re-thread them.

Initial Heading

The end section before the body of the rug begins is called the heading. It provides a firm base for a knotted fringe or a hem.

- Use two or three strands of the warp yarn wound together on the shuttle. See figure 1-5. The heading may be the same color as the warp or a combination of colors to blend with the rag strips.

- Weave a one-half to one-inch heading, or more if you wish, for a rug with a knotted fringe. It is very important to *allow ample slack* in each weft shot by laying weft threads in at an angle in order to prevent the heading from drawing in and distorting the shape of the rug. See figure 1-6.

Sampling the Weft

Cut several strips of fabric in different widths and weave a small sample with each size to determine the desired rag width. The rags should pack in firmly without too much bulk.

- The width of the rag strips will determine whether the rug will be pliable and thin or thick and heavy. Remember: *the less warp on the surface, the longer-wearing the rug.*

- An old "rule of thumb" guide for rag-cutting is: *a rag strip twisted between the fingers should be as thick as a pencil.* Using this adage as a guide, a lightweight fabric may be cut three inches wide, while a heavy wool should be only one-half inch. Cotton or a cotton blend fabric is usually cut one to two inches wide.

Preparing the Rags

After sampling with strips of various widths and determining the correct rag strip width for your project, prepare all the rags for the rug.

- Cut the strips using scissors or a rag cutter, or tear them along the length of the fabric. Sew strips together by overlapping and machine stitching. See figure 1-7. There are many short cuts and techniques for cutting and joining rags. See *Chapter Two* for other methods not shown here.

- Rags can be stored in bags if the sewing thread between joins is not cut. Some weavers prefer to wind the rags in balls. Balls may be all of one color, one fabric, or "hit-and-miss". Winding rags in balls is necessary only if you are taking them to someone else to weave.

- *To wind the rags on shuttles*: Start by loosely tying the rag at one end of the shuttle and wind until the shuttle is full but not bulging. A shuttle that is too full slows weaving because it must be pushed laboriously through the weaving shed.

- Some weavers like to have from six to ten shuttles ready so that all the rags can be wound on before starting to weave. Others prefer to hand feed the rags into the sheds. Either way, use your fingers to fold in frayed edges and to tuck in bulky joins and the beginning ends.

Beginning the Rug

Now start to weave with your rags.

1. *Open the shed, insert the shuttle*, angling the rag strip. See figure 1-8. Tuck in the beginning end, close the shed and beat at the same time, then beat again. At least two sharp beats are necessary, sometimes more. If packing seems difficult, it may help to raise all the shafts and beat.

2. *Change the shed and insert the shuttle again*. Angle the rag in each shed and twist it once at the selvedge to help it turn the corner snugly. The rag strip should *travel around* the end warp, without forming "ears" or loops. See figure 1-9.

To change shuttles: When joining rags between shuttles, taper the ends and overlap them in the shed for two to three inches. When one color of a stripe ends at the selvedge, extend the end three inches and cut it to taper it. Fold the new color rag, which is blunt-cut, around the tapered end, tuck in at the selvedge, and beat in place. See figure 1-10.

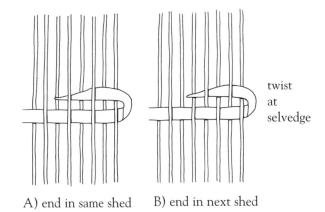

twist at selvedge

A) end in same shed   B) end in next shed

1-8. **Starting to weave.** Two methods of handling weft ends. A) Tuck end into the same shed. B) Tuck end into the next shed.

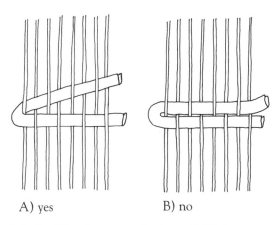

A) yes   B) no

1-9. **Avoiding loops at selvedges.** A) Weft snug against selvedge warp. B) Excess weft at selvedge.

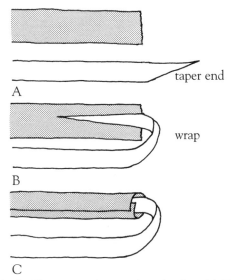

taper end

wrap

A

B

C

1-10. **Changing colors** at the selvedge. A) Taper end of old color. B) Wrap end of new color around tapered end. C) Completed color change.

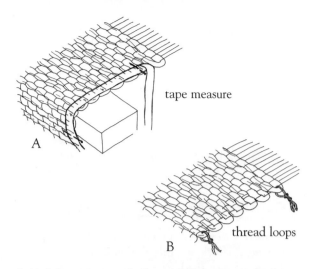

1-11. **Measuring methods.** A) Pin measuring tape to beginning of weaving and at intervals as rug progresses. B) Knot thread loops on selvedge warps at 13" intervals (12" + 1" take-up). Use one knot at first interval, 2 knots at second, etc.

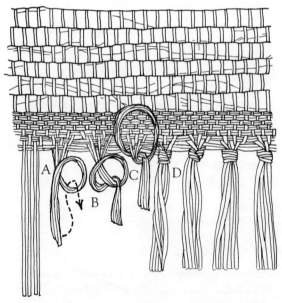

1-12. **Overhand knots.** Push open knots firmly against heading, then tighten.

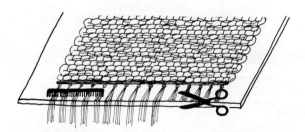

1-13. **Trimming the fringe** using table edge as a guide.

Measuring Your Progress

- Keep track of how much you have woven as you work. Two effective ways to measure, using a tape measure or thread loops, are illustrated. See figure 1-11. Keep the warp tight when measuring, and include the take-up allowance in your total measurement.

- Keep track of border and stripe designs as the work progresses. Many weavers clip a note to the front of the loom with notations such as "6 shots heading, 6 inches blue, 2 shots white, 4 inches red", etc.

Final Heading

When the rug is as long as desired, weave another heading to match the beginning and another two to three inches of scrap rags to hold the heading in place. Cut the rug off the loom allowing at least 5 to 6 inches of warp beyond the heading for a knotted fringe.

Basic Rug Finishing

A *knotted fringe* is the most common way to finish rag rugs. See figure 1-12. It is quick to tie and durable. (Instructions for a hemmed edge appear in *Chapter Two*.)

- Place the rug on a table or in your lap and very gently loosen the filler rags at one corner. Free the warp ends and tie groups of six with an overhand knot. Use your fingers to push the knot snugly against the heading. Loosen and free another bunch of warp ends and continue knotting. Repeat the process at the other end of the rug.

- Raveling the rag filler in small quantities will prevent the heading from loosening.

- *To trim the fringe:* lay the rug on a table or counter with the fringe extending slightly over the edge. See figure 1-13. Using fingers or a comb straighten the fringe and then cut, using the table edge as a guide for the scissors. A crack or seam in the table may also be used as a cutting guide.

Select Annotated Bibliography

Books

Collingwood, Peter. *The Techniques of Rug Weaving.* New York: Watson Guptill, 1968. This is the most complete reference on the craft of rug weaving. Although the emphasis is not on rag rugs, the mechanics of weaving and design are fully covered and many of the techniques lend themselves to fabric wefts as well as to wool or other materials.

Fredlund, Jane, and Birgit Wiberg. *Rag Rug Weaves: Patterns from Sweden.* Stockholm: LTs förlag, 1986. A small, short, practical guidebook with projects and many beautiful photographs of rag rugs in the Swedish tradition.

Ligon, Linda C., ed. *A Rug Weaver's Source Book.* Loveland, Colorado: Interweave Press, 1984. Written by eight different authors, this is a valuable rug text with two chapters on rag weaving.

Patrick, Jane, ed. *Just Rags, Handwoven's Design Collection Number 8.* Loveland, Colorado: Interweave Press, 1985. An inexpensive introduction to rag rugs, this softcover monograph explores rag weaving with photographs, projects, general instructions, and book list.

Tod, Osma Gallinger, and Josephine Couch Del Deo. *Designing and Making Handwoven Rugs.* New York: Dover Publications, 1976. A reprint by Dover Publications of the 1957 edition, this outstanding collection of rug information and projects devotes two chapters to rag rugs. Other sections serve as rich sources of inspiration.

Magazines

Handwoven. Interweave Press, 201 East Fourth Street, Loveland, CO 80537.

Shuttle, Spindle & Dyepot. Handweavers Guild of America, Two Executive Concourse, Suite 201, 3327 Duluth Highway, Duluth, GA 30096–3301.

Trade post card from the Newcomb Loom Company, ca. 1890. Promotion for the Newcomb Fly-shuttle Rag Carpet Loom appears on the reverse side, claiming "Any Person Can Use It." *Collection of Janet Meany.*

Chapter Two

Weaving Preparation

One of the especially fine things about weaving is [that] one can continue with it on into really old age—century mark and further. Not all the therapy is from the exercise and remuneration. One is creating—with the rag rugs—creating beauty and use from discarded materials. . . .

Mary B. Plaisted
The Shuttle, Spring 1964

FIRST NEWS OF THE NEWCOMB LOOM.

Warps

The choice of warp for a particular rug is determined by the type of rug desired, the rag quality, thread cost, and availability. *Remember that warp materials should be very strong, smooth, and resistant to abrasion.*

Suitable Warp Materials

The following are strong, durable threads of suitable diameter for rug warps. Sett recommendations are given in the chart.

Cotton Carpet Warp is recommended for the back door/kitchen sink rug in *Chapter One*. It is inexpensive, durable, and colorful. It is by far the most commonly used warp material and is suitable for most rugs. The 8/4 size consists of four strands of size 8 cotton twisted together.

Seine Twine is a particularly strong cotton warp made up of several double-plied strands of cotton.

4/4 Cotton consists of four strands of size 4 cotton. It is a heavier but not necessarily more durable warp.

Plain Butcher's String is similar to 8/4 cotton carpet warp.

Linen is naturally strong and smooth and makes an excellent warp. However, it is expensive and more difficult to tension evenly.

Synthetic Fibers such as polyester, nylon, and acrylic can also make good warps if they are strong, smooth, and not too elastic. Synthetic fibers fray less in the fringe than cotton and linen.

Type	Description	Sett
8/4 cotton carpet warp	inexpensive, widely available, washable, medium durability	10 or 12
4/4 cotton warp	heavier, fair durability	6 or 8
Linen 10/6 or 10/5	more expensive, less washable, natural color, very strong	5 or 6
Butcher's String	inexpensive, natural color	10 or 12
Seine Twine	more expensive and stronger than 8/4, very durable	6 or 10

Warp Setts

The *sett,* or number of *ends per inch (e.p.i.),* of a rug warp is determined by the characteristics of the warp yarn and by the desired "hand" of the rug. *Close setts* for rag rugs have warp ends sett at 10, 12, or 15 e.p.i. These setts are good for the finer-diameter warp yarns, and result in more warp ends showing on the rug surface. *Wide setts* such as 4, 6, or 8 e.p.i. are good for thicker warp materials, and result in more rag wefts showing on the rug surface.

A finer thread such as 8/4 cotton carpet warp is usually sett at 10 or 12 e.p.i. Heavier thread such as 10/5 linen may be sett at 5 or 6 e.p.i. Fine threads may be doubled and used at wider setts. For example, 8/4 carpet warp can be doubled and sett at 5 e.p.i. *In general, the wider the sett, the heavier the rug and the less friction or wear on the warp.*

Rag Weft Preparation

Once warp sett has been determined, you will need to weave a small sample with several different widths of rag strips to determine the kind of rug you want before cutting all the rags. See page 22 for sampling information.

Torn Strips

Tearing is probably the simplest method for making strips from large fabric pieces such as sheets and draperies. It is fast but very dusty and dirty work. It is best to wear a mask or work outdoors. To tear strips of even width, make small cuts at equal intervals along the shortest edge, hold the fabric so the cuts are along the top, then give a sharp tug at each cut.

Torn strips may appear ragged when woven. Sometimes this effect is desirable. If not, one of the cutting methods should be used.

Cut Strips

Several methods for cutting a single, long strip from a piece of fabric are shown in figures 2-1 through 2-5. Cuts should follow the *lengthwise grain* of the fabric whenever possible. Cutting cross-grain makes a ragged strip. Usually only long strips from clothing are practical to use; they make the best weaving rags. However, some weavers use all the fabric possible from clothing, including collars, pockets, and facings (sometimes even with buttons and buttonholes intact!).

Cutting rags

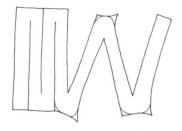

2-1. **Up-and-down method.** Cuts in flat fabric alternate from top and bottom edges.

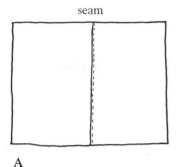

seam

2-2. **Tube method.** A) Seam two fabric widths. B) Seam into a tube. C) Make evenly-spaced cuts across tube. D) Make diagonal cuts connecting each slash to the next one.

A

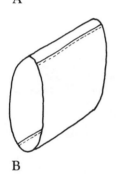

B

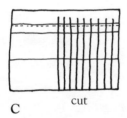

C

cut

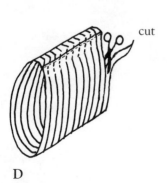

cut

D

A sharp scissors is essential for any of the following cutting methods. Scissors with a long blade such as those made for quilting or commercial sewing are a good investment for a rag rug weaver. If you are prone to blisters, it may be helpful to wear an old leather glove or use tape to cover "hot" spots on your hands.

• *Up-and-down method.* Make cuts alternately into the top and bottom of the fabric piece to within one inch of each edge. See figure 2-1.

• *Tube method.* Seam the fabric into a tube. See figure 2-2. Two fabric widths can be joined together for longer strips. Make evenly spaced slashes horizontally across the flattened tube to within 3 to 4 inches of the edge. Open the slashed tube and separate it into a continuous strip by making diagonal cuts connecting one strip to the next.

• *Circular method.* Round off the corners of a piece of fabric and cut into it in spiral fashion, working from the outside toward the center. See figure 2-3. A scissors or a wheel-type cutter and cutting board may be used for this method.

Cutting Tools

A variety of tools other than scissors make the work of cutting rag strips easier on the hands. Industrial power cutters of various sizes and models can be purchased from commercial sewing machine suppliers in major cities.

Olfa Cutter. This wheel device resembling a pizza cutter is available in two sizes. See figure 2-3. It cuts through many layers of fabric, and is used with its special plastic cutting board. It is often used with a straightedge, such as a yardstick, for a straighter cut.

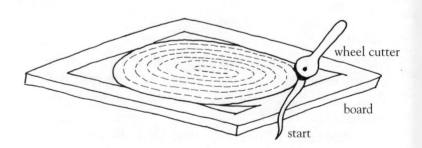

wheel cutter

board

start

2-3. **Circular method.** An Olfa cutter moves in a spiral cutting motion.

Fraser Rag Cutter. This rotary cutter is hand-cranked and adjustable for cuts of varying widths. See figure 2-4.

Butcher Knife. A sharp kitchen knife can slice off strips from tightly rolled fabric. See figure 2-5. Rolls can be dampened and frozen for easier slicing.

Paper Cutter. A standard office paper cutter can slice through folded fabric.

Power Saw. This tool can cut through many fabric layers.

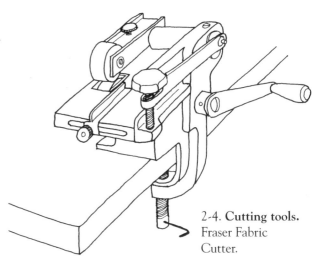

2-4. **Cutting tools.** Fraser Fabric Cutter.

Joining Rag Strips

There are as many ways to join strips as there are ways to cut strips. The method to use depends on the type of fabric and individual preference.

• *Bias join:* Place the first strip right-side up "east-west" on the sewing machine. Place the second strip wrong-side up on top of the first in a "north-south" position. Stitch diagonally across. Do not cut stitching thread. See figure 2-6A. Now place free end of top strip on top as before and stitch. By not cutting the thread between joins you will prevent tangling of the long strips and they can be stored until use. When ready to weave, trim the excess corners and snip threads.

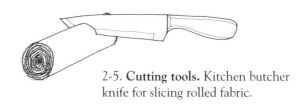

2-5. **Cutting tools.** Kitchen butcher knife for slicing rolled fabric.

• *Overlap and stitch:* Overlap blunt-cut ends one inch, fold in thirds and machine stitch a "smile" curve. Do not cut thread. Continue overlapping, folding, and stitching. See figure 2-6B.

• *Glue:* Fabric glue can be used to join strips. Even if it washes out, the strips will stay in place within the weaving if overlapped for several inches. Glue may stain light-colored fabrics, and it takes time to dry.

• *Laid-in:* If strips are very long it may not be necessary to sew them. Two ends may be overlapped in the same shed for *two inches* with the raw edges folded in on one another. Bulk can be reduced by tapering both ends with a bias cut. The joins that occur when changing shuttles are usually laid-in joins.

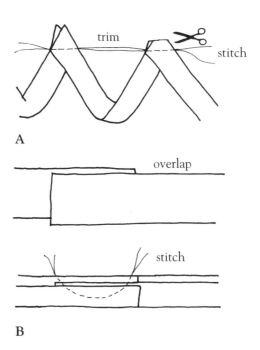

2-6. **Joining rags.** A) Bias join. B) "Smile" join.

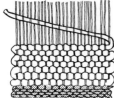

2-7. **Maintaining width.**
Angling the rag in the shed.

Rug Weaving Techniques

Selvedges

The selvedge probably causes more concern and provokes more discussion than any other aspect of rug weaving. Problems range from irregular selvedges to severe draw-in. Draw-in happens because the rag strip in the shed is not long enough to allow for the up-and-down journey it takes when traveling across the warp. While some selvedge irregularity is unavoidable, excessive draw-in results in a rug that has loose selvedges and is misshapen when cut off the loom.

There are several ways to build enough slack into each weft shot to avoid selvedge problems.

Always angle the rag in the shed. See figure 2-7. With every pick, lay the rag at an angle of approximately 30° from the selvedge toward the beater. The rag should exit the shed 6 to 8 inches above the fell line. Beat first with an open shed, then change the shed and beat again. *It will be necessary to advance the warp every 2 to 3 inches to allow enough working space.*

Use a stretcher or temple, a tool with prongs (nails) at the ends, that maintains the rug width. See figure 2-8. It is placed just below the fell line and needs to be advanced frequently.

Prevent curved ends by maintaining the 30° weft angle when weaving. Handle the selvedge threads as little as possible when turning the rag at the selvedge. Curving is the result of both draw-in and stretched selvedge warps, and usually disappears after several washings or after prolonged use. See figure 2-9.

Doubled selvedges. Many rug weavers double the last two warp ends on each selvedge for extra strength. If you wish to do this, add the extra ends when winding your warp. Draw them doubled through the last two heddles on each side and through the last two spaces in the reed at the selvedges of the rug.

2-8. **Temple or stretcher device.**

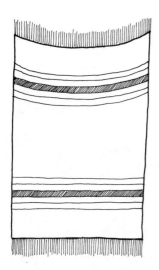

2-9. **Curved end** from stretched selvedge warps.

Filler

The filler rags or yarn used to spread the warp or hold the heading in place are easy to remove if woven in this fashion: Put in each filler pick by doubling it in in a back-and-forth motion, always entering the weft from the same side. See figure 2-10.

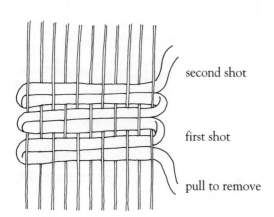

second shot

first shot

pull to remove

2-10. **Removing the filler** from the finished rug.

Heading Patterns

The two headings described below can be woven on a four-shaft loom threaded in twill weave.

Twill heading. Use two strands of carpet warp and weave heading in twill pattern. Treadle shafts 1 and 2 together, then 2 and 3, 3 and 4, and finally, 4 and 1.

Vertical stripe heading. Use two shuttles, each wound with a single strand of contrasting-color carpet warp. Vertical stripes will result.

- Treadle shafts 1 and 2 together and weave one color.
- Treadle shafts 3 and 4 together and weave the other color. Use a fork to aid in pressing the weft to cover the warp completely.

Hints for Headings

- *Match the heading color* to the rag color so there isn't a surprise stripe at the ends of the rug. Sometimes it works well to use two or three different colors together in a multicolored heading. This heading is also a good way to use up leftover warp thread.
- *Double the heading thread.* Use doubled or tripled warp thread to weave the heading, as in figure 1-5. Headings woven with a single strand of carpet warp tend to draw in severely. Allow plenty of weft in each shed to prevent draw-in.
- *Twining.* A row of weft twining may be worked across the width before starting the heading. See figure 2-11. Fold a *2-yard* piece of warp thread in half over the first warp end and twist the two ends around each warp end. Knot ends at last warp. The firm edge of the twining provides extra insurance against raveling. Caution: To avoid draw-in, do not pull twining thread too tightly.

Hints for Rag Wefts

- *Fraying.* If the rag fabric frays easily, it may be desirable to fold in raw edges at the selvedges. Some weavers fold all of the raw edges under.
- *Narrow strips.* Some weavers favor using several narrow strips wound together on the shuttle instead of a single, wide strip. With several strips, the weft packs in more securely and interesting color patterns develop.
- *Color blending with narrow strips.* You can achieve subtle color blends by using two *half-inch* rag strips in place of single *one-inch* strips. To shade from blue to white, for example, use two strips of blue weft for 2",

I notice some of the weavers speak of their trouble with the edges of their rugs. The lady who taught me how to weave showed me a simple little trick and I have never had the slightest unevenness and I have never used one of those gadgets with pins in the ends to stretch the rugs [a temple]. The trick is simply this: When you put in your rags, let them lay across the warp three or four inches. When you beat them in, this little extra comes into shape easily. [If] you lay the rags straight across, when they are beaten in they pull the warp in tight and will cause an uneven edge. Learn to lay the rags in this way each time across and your rugs will finish very nicely.

Mrs. Don F. Cooley
The Shuttle, 1963

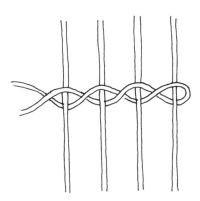

2-11. **Twining.** Fold a length of warp thread around the first warp. Cross the two ends between each warp across the width. Knot ends together to finish.

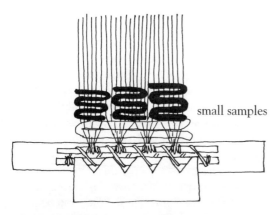

small samples

2-12. **Sampling for rag width.** Several small samples worked across the web.

one blue and one white for 2", then white strips until you want to change the color again.

Two-shuttle weaving. When using two shuttles, lock the wefts at the selvedges as follows: When both shuttles are on the same side, change the shed and look at the last warp on that side. If the thread is up, pass the next shuttle *over* the other shuttle and into the shed. If the thread is down, pass the next shuttle *under* the other shuttle.

Sampling

A good way to sample the width of rags is to weave several small patches of rugs across the width of your warp. They are quick to weave and remove and provide a good sampling of how various rags will weave up. See figure 2-12.

Removing Rugs from the Loom

The thick build-up of fabric on the cloth beam often makes it necessary to remove rugs before the entire warp is woven. On most looms there is room for only six to eight finished rugs on the cloth beam, while the warp beam can accommodate yardage for many more rugs. A group of rugs can be cut off the loom and weaving resumed without retying the warp ends to the apron bar.

To cut off, release the tension and unroll the finished rugs. Untie the warp from the front apron bar. Cut through the warp between the last two rugs. *Leave the last rug on the loom* and wrap it evenly around the cloth beam by hand.

To start a new rug, turn the cloth advance until the last rug is entirely wrapped around the beam and the warp is exposed.

Reweaving

It is possible to reweave rags when a rug's warp has worn out. Wash the old rug first, then unravel it, cutting through the warp occasionally. Wind the rags in a ball or directly onto shuttles and use them to weave a new rug.

Finishing Techniques

After the rug is cut from the loom, a finish must be applied to prevent raveling. Hems and fringe are the two most common finishes.

Hemmed Finish

While fringe is the most popular rug finish, it wears away after repeated washings. Machine drying is particularly hard on fringe. A hemmed finish, on the other hand, wears longer and is easy to do.

Hems require at least two inches of heading woven at each end of the rug. After cutting the rug off the loom, machine stitch the heading securely and fold it back on itself to form a triple-layer hem. See figure 2-13.

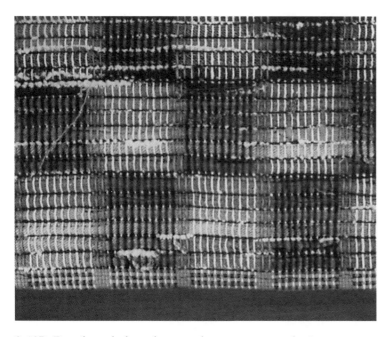

2-13B. Detail, triple-layer hem on denim rug woven by Janet Meany.

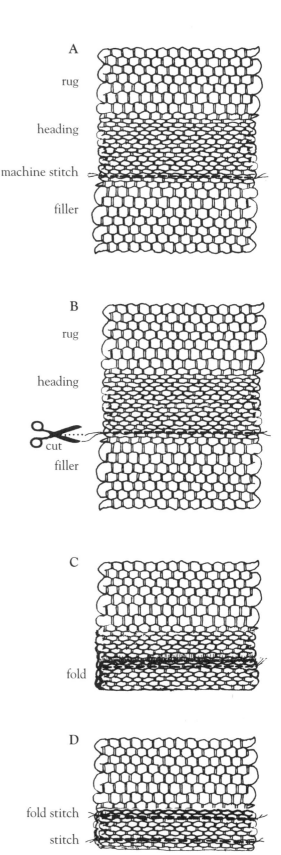

2-13A. **Triple-layer hem.** A) Machine stitch heading at hem edge. B) Cut away filler. C) Fold up 1/3 of hem and stitch. D) Fold again and stitch hem in place.

23

Decorative Fringe Finishes

Fringe is formed of groups of 4, 6, or 8 warp ends tied together with overhand knots. Knotting fringe more than once makes it last longer and look tidier. Allow *five to six inches* of warp at each end of a rug for working fringe.

• *Crossed warps.* Exchange the end threads in each knotted group to lock the weft firmly in place. See figure 2-14.

• *Plied warps.* Overtwist the warps, combine them, and then twist in the opposite direction. See figure 2-15.

• *Three-strand braid.* Braid and knot the fringe to add thickness and durability. See figure 2-16.

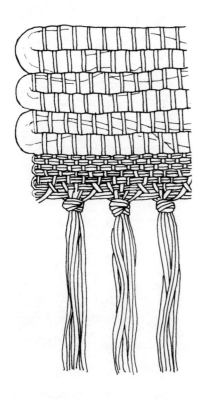

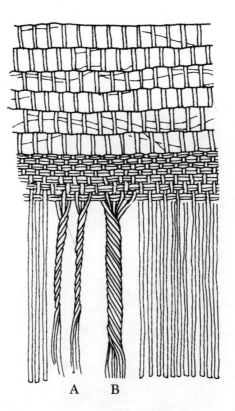

A   B

2-14. **Crossed warps.** Cross warps between each knotted group.

2-15. **Plied warps.** A) Twist two groups of warps *tightly* in the same direction. B) Place the two groups together and twist in the opposite direction. Knot the ends together.

2-16. **Three-strand braid.** Cross each outer strand over the center strand.

- *Alternating overhand knots.* Vary the overhand knot edge by adding a staggered second row and repeating as desired. See figure 2-17.
- *Double-knot variation.* A decorative variation of the alternating overhand knot edging is made by interlacing groups of warp and knotting again. See figure 2-18.
- *Multiple knots.* A series of overhand knots in a single warp group thickens the fringe. See figure 2-19.

Trimming Fringes

A wheel-type rag cutter, such as the Olfa cutter, is an excellent tool for trimming fringes. Comb out the fringe on the cutting board and cut across using a straightedge as a guide.

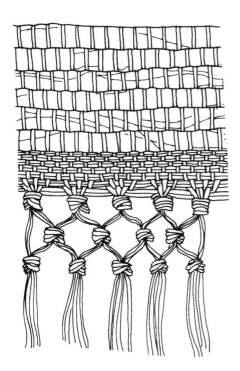

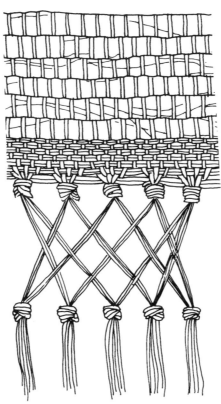

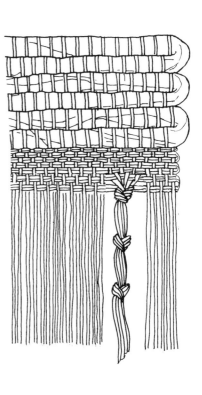

2-17. **Alternating overhand knots.** Tie one row of overhand knots across the rug. Divide the warps from each knot in half, combine, and knot again. Repeat as desired.

2-18. **Double-knot variation.** Tie one row of overhand knots across warp. Interweave the warp groups before tying the second row of knots.

2-19. **Multiple knots.** Tie a series of overhand knots in the same warp groups.

Opposite. Cover photo from *The Shuttle*, magazine for members of the Maysville Guild of Home Weavers, September 1942.

While clearing out my sister-in-law's house, I found a bag of polyester scraps. Here was a thirty-year accumulation of remnants, pieces cut from skirts and pants, hems of clothing she had received as gifts from her children. I wove a rag rug on natural-colored warp with these bright pieces and called it 'Mother's Hems'.

Mildred Carselle
St. Paul, Minnesota

Chapter Three

What Now? Designing Plain Weave Rag Rugs

Photo by La Vern Duemey

SEPTEMBER 1942

Cover: Mrs. E. T. Miller. See Page 3 for her story.

27

Rag rug designs based on plain weave fit into three categories. The first includes rugs woven on a solid-color warp where the rag colors dominate the design. The second includes rugs woven on multicolored warps whose colors contribute significantly to the rug's overall color composition. In the third category, both warp and weft have equal design emphasis. This category includes plaids, checkerboards, and the traditional *Log Cabin* weaves.

When planning, make a small sketch of the proposed rug with colored pencils or pens. To indicate proportions, draw out the stripes or plaids on a large piece of paper exactly to size. Some weavers experiment with the color arrangement of the rag strips, either by laying them out on a table or by moving them around the warp on the loom until they find a pleasing arrangement.

Planning Sett

The *warp sett* determines the durability of a rag rug and influences the appearance of the weave. If warp ends are sett at 10 or 12 ends per inch, more warp will show on the surface of the rug than if the warp is sett at 4, 6, or 8 ends per inch. Rugs woven on wider setts have most of the warp protected by the rags and wear longer than those with more warp exposed.

Single warp ends are shown in figure 3-1. Figure 3-2 shows warp ends doubled and sett at wider setts (4, 6, or 8 doubled ends per inch) for greater strength.

The warp ends may be doubled two ways:

• *Double-threading*. Thread two ends together as one in the heddles and in the reed.

• *Doubling by treadling*. If the heddles are threaded 1,2,3,4,1,2,3,4 on a four-shaft loom and a wider sett is desired, treadling shafts 1 and 2 together and 3 and 4 together will yield a doubled warp in the weaving.

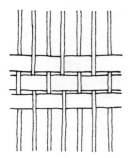

3-1. **Single warp ends** in a close sett.

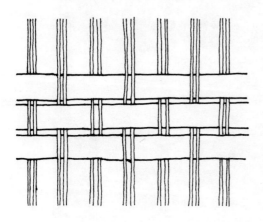

3-2. **Doubled warp ends** in a wide sett.

Plain Weave Rugs with Weft Emphasis

Use a wider sett for these weaves that show weft colors to best advantage.

Hit-and-Miss

This lively, multicolored pattern results from using fabrics of many colors and patterns in no particular order. The length of the strips and the angle of the joins can produce interesting pattern effects, particularly if the fabric is composed of solid colors. See figure 3-3; *Projects 1, 2, 3, and 20.* For hit-and-miss patterns, one source suggests that the strips sewn together should not be longer than eighteen inches. To avoid a stripe effect, another rug maker weaves with pieces that do not exceed two yards in length. Others use two or three rows of a fabric with four or five (or more) different fabrics used in sequence throughout the rug.

Here is one common hit-and-miss method:

1. Divide the rag strips into piles or bags by color; by light, medium, and dark; by prints, plaids, and solids.

2. When sewing rags together, arrange the piles or bags in order. Take one strip from each pile in sequence to join. When woven, the colors, shades, or patterns will be evenly distributed throughout the rug in a hit-and-miss fashion.

A more regular hit-and-miss pattern results from joining several lengths of fabrics of various colors into a tube then cutting as described in *Project 2*. Because each fabric reappears in the same length and in the same sequence, an interesting design emerges.

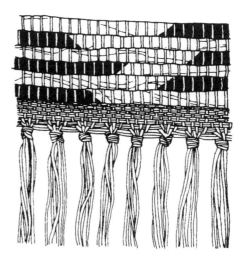

3-3. **Angled joins** as design element in a hit-and-miss rug.

Stripes

Rag colors may be woven in horizontal stripes that begin and end at the selvedges. These stripes may border either end of the rug or they may form a continuous succession of colors and/or patterns throughout. While ten stripe patterns are illustrated in figure 3-4, there are endless possibilities for designing such patterns, both symmetrical and asymmetrical.

• *Symmetrical stripes*. If the stripes are to be the same at both ends of the rug, divide the rags into two equal parts so that there will be enough of each kind to complete the design. Keep a written record of the number of rows of each color so that you can repeat the same sequence at the other end.

• *Wide stripes*. These can be broken up by placing other colors within them, as in figures 3-4A and 3-4B. They can also be accented with a bright, narrow stripe on either side. See figure 3-4C. One or two horizontal stripes at either end may border a center area of hit-and-miss. See figure 3-4D. If you use figured materials in the body of the rug, it might be well to use solid-color stripes for the end borders. See figure 3-5.

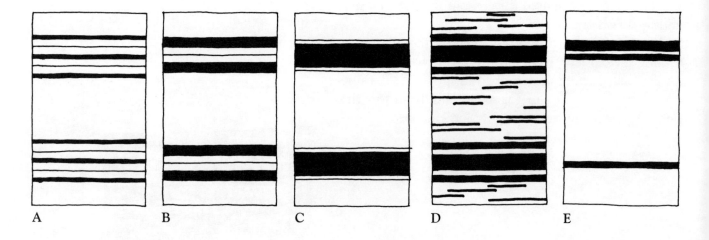

A   B   C   D   E

3-4. **Weft stripe arrangements.** A) Wide stripe arrangement with center accent. B) Wide and narrow stripe arrangement. C) Bordered stripe. D) Striped borders, hit-and-miss center. E) Asymmetrical arrangement. F) Regular arrangement. G) Repeated pattern. H) Borders. I) Blended stripe between two colors. J) Graduated stripe.

• *Asymmetrical stripes.* Swedish rag rug books are filled with a variety of weft stripe designs, many asymmetrical. Anything goes! See figure 3-4E.

Dyed Stripe Variations

Stripes can be dyed into rags in various ways. Here are two methods.

• *Rainbow.* Beautifully shaded "rainbow" rugs are fun to weave. Dye sheets or large fabric pieces many different colors and shades, then weave the resulting strips in a particular order throughout the rug, or in a random manner. *Log Cabin* threading works well as warp for a rainbow rug. See *Project 5.*

• *Ikat.* Fabric strips may be ikat, or resist-dyed, to create interesting shadowy patterns. See figure 3-6. Join fabric strips and wind into a skein. Bind resist sections tightly with plastic and put the skeins into a dye bath. The areas not bound with plastic will take the dye.

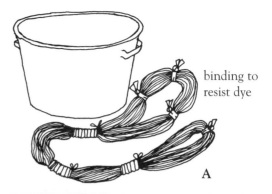

binding to resist dye

A

B

3-6. **Ikat.** A) Skein of fabric strips bound for ikat dyeing. B) Detail, ikat rug designed and woven by Mary Anne Wise, Stockholm, Wisconsin.

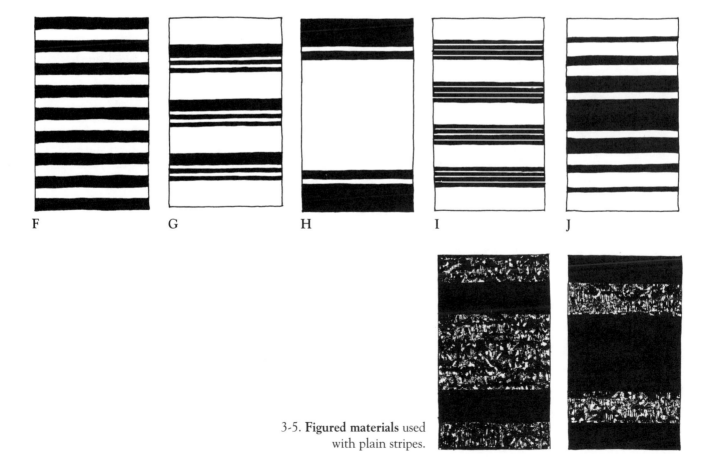

F   G   H   I   J

3-5. **Figured materials** used with plain stripes.

3-7A. **Twisted wefts.** S- and Z-twists.

Twisted Wefts

Shaker weavers frequently used the twisted weft technique. It makes an interesting "mottled" pattern. Twisting the rags toward the left results in an S-twist; twisting them toward the right produces a Z-twist. See figure 3-7A. A large quantity of rags may be twisted on a spinning wheel.

To weave a twisted pattern area:

1. *Wind a shuttle* with two narrow strips of contrasting color rags and put it through the shed.

2. *Twist them in one direction* so that diagonals appear.

3. *Change the shed* to lock the twists in place before beating.

4. In the next row, twist the strips in the same direction for a "twill" effect, or in the opposite direction for an "arrow" pattern. Experiment with the directions of the twist and the number of rows woven with each type.

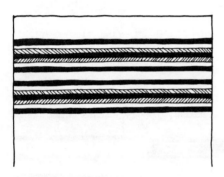

3-7B. **Herringbone or Feather Stripe Border.**

Twisted Border Patterns

Directions for two twisted border stripes published in an early Deen Loom Catalogue are reprinted below. See figures 3-7B and 3-7C. The body of each rug is woven in black-and-white strips twisted together.

- *Herringbone or Feather Stripe Border.*
1. First band: Weave six inches of black-and-white twisted together (or plain rags).
2. Pattern rows:
   1 shot black
   2 shots white
   2 shots black-and-white Z-twist
   1 shot black
   2 shots black-and-white S-twist
   2 shots white
   1 shot black

3. Weave four inches black-and-white twisted (or plain) rags.

4. Repeat stripe and continue to weave the body of rug, finishing with two stripes at the other end.

- *Herringbone and Sawtooth Border.*

1. Weave 6 inches black-and-white twisted (or plain rags).

2. Pattern rows:
   1 shot black
   2 shots white
   2 shots black-and-white Z-twist
   1 shot black
   2 shots black-and-white S-twist
   4 shots white
   2 shots black-and-white Z-twist
   4 shots black
   2 shots black-and-white Z-twist
   2 shots white
   2 shots black-and-white S-twist
   4 shots black
   2 shots black-and-white S-twist
   4 shots white
   2 shots black-and-white Z-twist
   1 shot black
   2 shots black-and-white S-twist
   2 shots white
   1 shot black

3. Weave the body of the rug. Finish at the other end with the same design.

3-7C. **Herringbone and Sawtooth Border.**

3-7D. **Detail, Twisted Border Rug,** collection of Mildred Carselle, St. Paul, Minnesota.

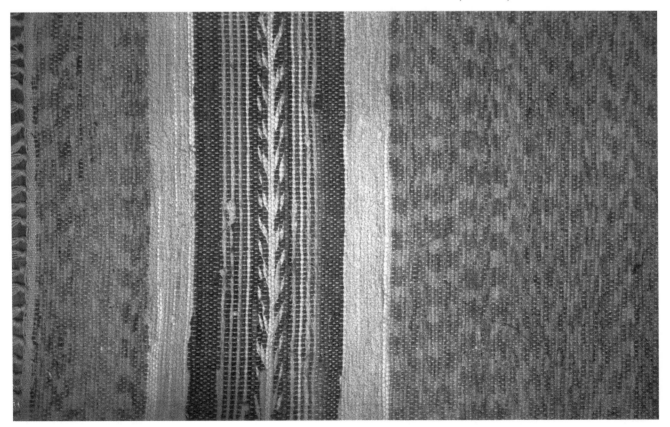

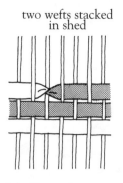

two wefts stacked
in shed

3-8. **Two-color twisting.**
Two colors placed on top
of each other on the
shuttle twisted to bring
the bottom color to the
surface.

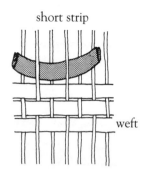

short strip

weft

3-9. **Laid-in.** Short
strips added to the
shed.

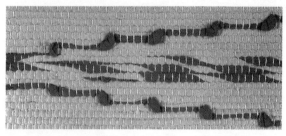

3-10. **Diagonal pattern** formed by carrying laid-in
weft from row to row. Woven by Irja Wattunen.

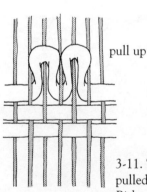

pull up

3-11. **Tufting.** *Left:* Weft loops
pulled up between warps.
Right: Detail, tufted rug by
Paula Pfaff.

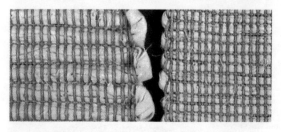

3-12. **Ribbed weave** detail. The ribbed effect is
more dramatic with greater contrast between the
thick and thin wefts. Woven by Paula Pfaff.

Twist Variation with Doubled Strips

For another twist effect, put strips of two different
colors on the same shuttle, stacked one on top of the
other. While laying them in the shed, twist the strips
to change color. See figure 3-8. You can control the
placement of colors in this way. Change the shed to
lock the twist in place before beating. A fabric like cal-
ico or drapery material printed on just one side may be
used in place of two different color strips.

Laid-In

Laying short pieces of fabric into the shed on top of
the regular weft shot creates irregular areas of color and
texture. Figurative designs can be made by laying in
pieces of various short lengths to follow a chart or
drawing. If the ends of the laid-in strips are allowed to
protrude, they give the appearance of pile. See figure
3-9. For a different sort of accent, a longer strip may be
carried from row to row over the surface of the rug,
making a diagonal laid-in weft design. See figure 3-10.

Tufting

You may vary plain-weave areas with picked-up
loops or tufting. Pass the weft loosely through the shed,
then pull up loops between the warp ends. See figure
3-11. Pull up loops of varying heights. Use the loops to
form rows or isolated areas of texture. Leave the loops
as they are, or clip them for a tufted effect. Add several rows of plain weave between the tufts to hold them
in place.

Ribbed Weave

A heavy, ribbed texture is achieved by alternating
wefts of rags and carpet warp. Use two shuttles, one
wound with rags and the other wound with carpet
warp. Enter them alternately into the sheds. See figure
3-12. For a maximum ribbing effect, employ strong

contrast in the thickness of the wefts. Instructions are given below for one type of ribbed rug. Another type appears in *Project 8.*

1. Put black warp on shafts 1 and 3 (or shaft 1) and colored warp on shafts 2 and 4 (or shaft 2).

2. Weave alternating shots of carpet warp and rags. The black warp will cover the fine weft and the colors will cover the rags.

3. *To change the warp color sequence,* weave two rows of rags, then resume the alternation in step 2. Now the colors will cover the fine weft and the black warp will cover the rags.

Tapestry Weave

The weft is manipulated by hand in tapestry weaving. There can be many color changes in each row. See figure 3-13. Usually, the warp ends are widely sett (4, 5, or 6 e.p.i.) and fabric strips may be used in place of yarn. Most rug weaving books provide information on tapestry weaves and methods of joining color areas. (See Collingwood's *The Techniques of Rug Weaving.*)

Clasped Wefts

This random pattern adds an interesting surface texture to rag rugs.

1. *Use two narrow, contrasting rag wefts.* Wind one into a ball and place it in a basket or other container. Wind the other on a shuttle.

2. Push the shuttle through the shed and loop it around the other weft, then return it to its own side. See figure 3-14A. The weft is doubled in that row and a loop is formed where the two wefts "clasp". See figure 3-14B. As you continue weaving, the loops may be placed at random or arranged in a deliberate sequence to form a design. See figure 3-14C.

Clasped Wefts and Ribs

For a variation in the ribbed technique, loop contrasting wefts of carpet warp. These thin clasped wefts can be placed between shots of thicker rags for an interesting design element.

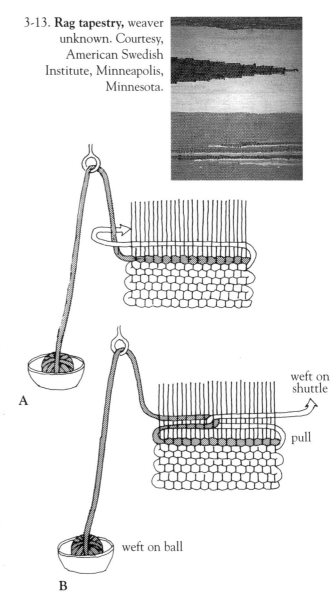

3-13. **Rag tapestry,** weaver unknown. Courtesy, American Swedish Institute, Minneapolis, Minnesota.

weft on shuttle

pull

A

weft on ball

B

C

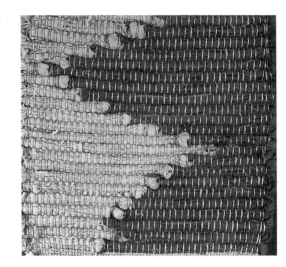

3-14. **Clasped wefts.** A) The shuttle weft reaches through the shed to clasp the balled weft. B) Placement of clasped join in the shed. C) Detail of looped effect.

Plain Weave Rugs with Warp Emphasis

These patterns call for dominant warp colors and plain or neutral rag colors. Use a close sett to emphasize the warp.

Warp Stripes

As with weft stripes, there are endless possibilities. Ten warp stripe arrangements are shown in figure 3-15. For inspiration, look at fabric swatches or striped patterns in magazines. Sketch stripes with colored pencils or pens when planning the warp.

Stripes may be wound directly into the warp. See Appendix I for general warping directions. For example, wind 24 ends of red on the warping board or reel, then cut the thread at the end of the warp and attach the next color, white, with an overhand knot. Wind 10 white. Cut and tie on the next color in the sequence.

• *Simple stripes.* Wind your warp with a border of one or more stripes on each side of the rug. See figure 3-15A. You may also place stripes all the way across. See figure 3-15B. The stripes can consist of two or more colors.

• *Blended stripes.* A stripe of blended colors between solid colors is an interesting variation. See figure 3-15C. Wind one stripe in a solid color (for

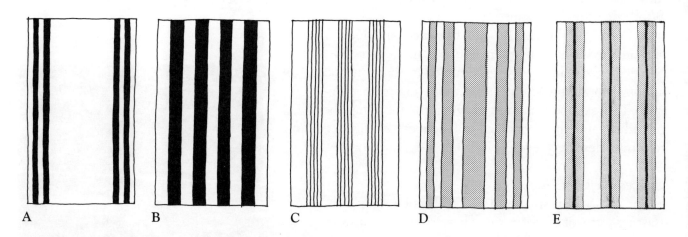

A   B   C   D   E

3-15. **Warp stripes.** A) Border stripes. B) Regular stripes. C) Blended stripes. D) Graduated stripes. E) Wide stripes with narrow band. F) E stripes crossed with hit-and-miss. G) Doubled warp stripes. H) Warp divided into five sectors with light and dark arrangements. I) Border stripe on four sides. J) Plaid.

example, red) and next to that, wind a stripe with two close colors (for example, red and orange). Wind the next stripe with the lighter solid (orange) and repeat the pattern.

• *Border stripe on four sides.* For a colored border all around the rug, make a contrasting-color stripe in the warp at each side. Wind twice the number of threads normally used for the stripe width, and double-sley them in the reed (two ends per dent). The body of the rug can be sett normally. See figure 3-15I. Weave a rag border at each end of the rug to match the warp stripe in color and in width.

• *Multicolor warp variations.*

A) Shaded. Divide the warp into five sections: two dark colors alternating; two light colors alternating; two dark; two light; two dark again. See figure 3-15H. Weave with fabric strips all one color or in stripes.

B) Mottled. Put one color on shaft 1 (shafts 1 and 3) across, and two or more colors on shaft 2 (shafts 2 and 4). Weave as usual with fabric strips. A shot of rag covered by solid-color warp alternates with a shot of rag covered by multicolored warps.

For another way to achieve a mottled effect, see *Ribbed Weave*, page 34.

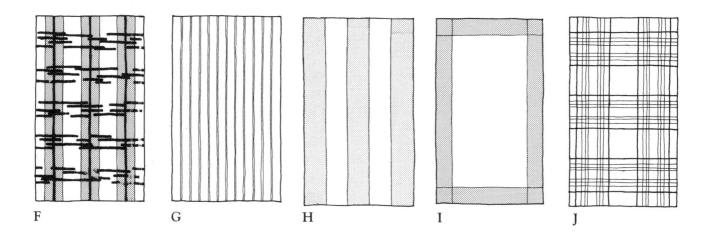

F   G   H   I   J

10 e.p.i.   10 e.p.i.   30 e.p.i.

2 colors, 10 ends each

3-16. **Clustered warp.** Warp Rep Stripes and Squares pattern. Woven by Paula Pfaff.

Random Warp

A random warp is a multicolored warp in which there is no set color order. A single end of one color might be followed by several ends of another color. A "salt and pepper" effect results when an odd number of colors are threaded singly in sequence. Random warps are a good way to use small amounts of leftover warp.

Clustered Warp

Achieve a richly textured surface by threading the heddles with the full amount of warp in the regular order, and sleying the reed with four ends in one dent and none in the next three. The rug will have a "puffed" appearance between the clustered warps or warp rep stripes.

• *Warp Rep Stripes and Squares.* For this pattern, the warp is sett very close in certain sections to produce a vertical stripe accent. If contrasting colors are alternated in the stripe areas only, there will be a "checkerboard" effect in each stripe. See figure 3-16.

The warps must be dense enough to cover the weft for this technique to be successful. As many as 30 e.p.i. should be sleyed for the dense warp stripes. Additional accent stripes, also sett very closely, may be added on either side of the larger warp stripes. The remainder of the rug may be sleyed at the usual number of ends per inch.

• *All-over Effect.* Double the warp ends at two- or three-inch intervals all the way across the width of the warp. See figure 3-15G.

Plain Weave Rugs with Warp and Weft Emphasis

Color arrangements in the warp and weft, plus closer warp setts, produce these lively patterns.

Plaid

A plaid has two or more colors in both warp and weft. The colored warp stripes are crossed by colored weft stripes. For a balanced plaid, the weft stripes should be woven in the same succession of colors as the warp stripes. See figure 3-15J. Interesting effects occur when the weft color sequence is varied.

Commercial fabrics can provide inspiration for colorful and varied plaids. Tartan weaves, in particular, are a good source of ideas.

Checkerboard

Checkerboard motifs are a variation on plaid. See *Project 4*. The Newcomb Loom Company catalogue *Series B, The Improved No. 3* suggests the following way to weave a checkerboard:

1. Use two colors of warp set up in four-inch wide stripes. Between each band of color put in two ends of red for a fine line, four for a more defined stripe.

2. Use all solid colors in the weft. A red border will be formed around each square. See figure 3-17. Weaving sequence:

4 inches rag color 1
4 shots red warp
4 inches rag color 2
4 shots red warp.

Log Cabin

The Log Cabin arrangement of warp threads has long been handed down from mother to daughter and shared throughout communities. While instruction books call it "Honeycomb", it has no resemblance to the four-shaft traditional Honeycomb weave. See *Project 5*.

Given the rich array of fabrics and warp colors available, Log Cabin threading can modify and enhance

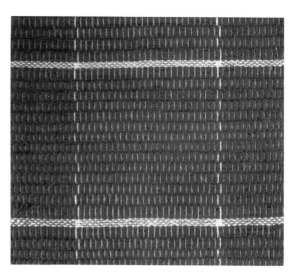

3-17. **Checkerboard** detail, woven by Paula Pfaff.

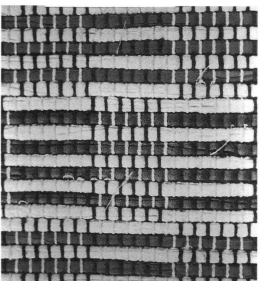

color change

color change

3-18. **Log Cabin** pattern using two shots of white weft to change the block. Woven by Helga Johnson, Two Harbors, Minnesota.

the surface of a rug in almost limitless ways.

Log Cabin is two-shaft weave but it can be threaded on as many shafts as are on the loom. Threads of two contrasting colors alternate in the warp. Black and white are the traditional favorites. The order of the colors changes at each block area:

1. *Alternate black and white* for 12 threads (one inch).
2. *Reverse the order* to white and black for 12 threads.
3. Continue to alternate colors in blocks. Two black threads or two white threads will be adjacent after every 12 warp ends. See figure 3-18.

Variations on the Log Cabin weave include using thick and thin wefts, varying the colors of the weft and warp, and creating blocks, bricks, and larger areas of design. See *Projects 6-11*. Stripes of Log Cabin alternating with stripes of solid-color warp create an interesting composition. See *Project 12*.

Twill Rugs

The four-shaft twill weave is very popular for rag rugs. In twill, raising the shafts in a paired sequence (1 and 2, 2 and 3, 3 and 4, 4 and 1) creates a diagonal arrangement of warp threads on the surface. See figure 3-19. Four twill weave rugs are included for four-shaft weavers. See *Projects 13, 14, 16, 17*.

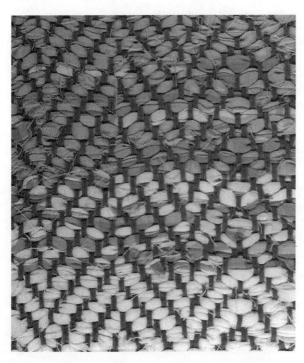

3-19. **Twill weave.** Woven by Paula Pfaff.

Opposite. Cover, Deen Loom Company catalog, ca. 1925, featuring the company's line of fly-shuttle looms and promoting rag rug weaving as a profitable home business.

My loom may be loud but I'll tell you. That loom sang to me. It sang 'food on the table, shoes for the kid'.

Irja Wattunen
Winton, Minnesota

Chapter Four

Projects

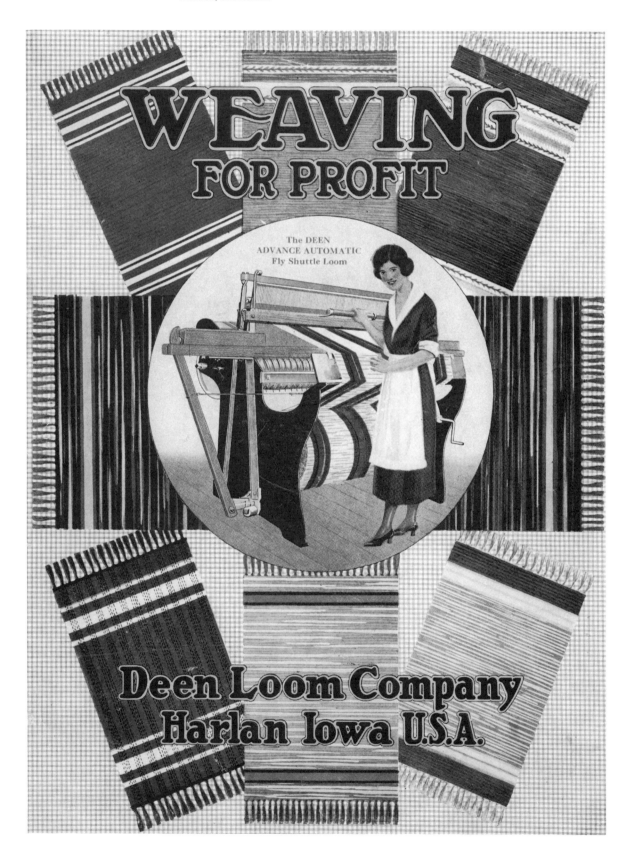

41

Preface to Projects: Reading a Draft

Everyone needs ideas to get started. To satisfy those needs we have selected twenty rag rugs for which detailed instructions are provided. The first projects are in plain weave. Succeeding ones increase in complexity. We present several versions of the popular *Log Cabin Pattern*, both plain and with stripes. In the four-shaft category are some favorite patterns from old loom instruction manuals: *Double Seed*, *The Anderson Weave*, and *The Hollywood Weave*. Two reversible rugs, a reversible twill, and *Swedish Double Binding* are also included. For those wishing to carpet a room with rag rugs, there is a room-sized rag rug project.

In order to use these instructions, the beginning weaver needs to learn how to read a *threading draft*. The system outlined here is similar to that found in many instruction books. For more detailed information, consult a standard weaving text.

Threading

A threading draft is usually diagrammed on graph paper. It is read and threaded from right to left. Each X represents one warp end. The shafts are numbered at the right of the draft. The X is shown on the shaft on which the end is threaded. The shaft at the front of the loom is Number 1; the second, Number 2, etc.

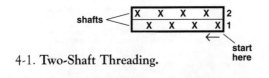

4-1. **Two-Shaft Threading.**

Two-Shaft Draft

The first X in figure 4-1 shows a warp end that passes through the first heddle on shaft 1. The second end passes through the first heddle on shaft 2. Continue threading the heddles all the way across according to the threading draft.

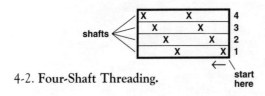

4-2. **Four-Shaft Threading.**

Four-Shaft Draft

A loom may have two or four shafts (or more). In figure 4-2 the first warp end goes through the heddle on shaft 1, the second end on shaft 2, the third end on shaft 3, and the fourth end on shaft 4.

Many project rugs can be woven on a two-shaft loom. A glance at the threading draft will show you how many shafts each pattern requires.

Tie-Up

The tie-up is found at the far right of the draft. It refers to the way in which the treadles are fastened to the shafts. The tie-up symbol O is normally used to indicate each shaft of a jack loom (rising shed loom). The symbol X shows shafts on a counterbalanced loom (sinking shed loom). The drafts in these projects use the O symbol for the jack loom. If you have a counterbalanced loom, put an X in each empty square and tie accordingly.

Direct Tie-Up

Figure 4-3 shows a *direct tie-up* for a two-shaft loom. Each shaft is attached to only one treadle. Treadle 1 is tied to shaft 1, treadle 2 is tied to shaft 2. A 4-shaft draft for a direct tie-up is shown in figure 4-4.

Standard Tie-Up

A tie-up for raising more than one shaft with one treadle is shown in figure 4-5. This can be done on a loom that has *lamms* between the treadles and the shafts. Treadle 1 is attached to shafts 1 and 3, treadle 2 is attached to shafts 2 and 4. Plain weave or *tabby* is produced on a four-shaft loom set up in this manner.

Treadling

The treadling draft is located above the tie-up and shows the weaving plan. For plain weave (tabby), figure 4-6 shows the two-shaft weave plan, figure 4-7 shows the four-shaft plan. Read treadling order from bottom to top. Figure 4-6 shows that you step on treadle 1 (raise shaft 1) and weave. Then step on treadle 2 (raise shaft 2) and weave. Twill weave treadling is shown in figure 4-8.

When starting a new pattern, look first at the threading, then the tie-up, and then the treadling.

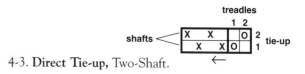

4-3. **Direct Tie-up**, Two-Shaft.

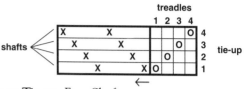

4-4. **Direct Tie-up**, Four-Shaft.

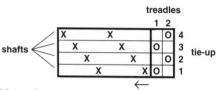

4-5. **Tie-up Using Lamms.**

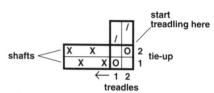

4-6. **Tabby Treadling**, Two-Shaft.

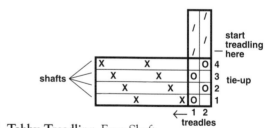

4-7. **Tabby Treadling**, Four-Shaft.

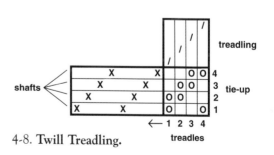

4-8. **Twill Treadling.**

43

Color Plates *(Pages 45 to 48)*

Plate 1. Landscape Rug woven by Missy Stevens, Washington, Connecticut. An innovative inlay technique using cotton and corduroy strips. *Photo by William Bennet Seitz.*

Plate 2. Winter Sunset Rug woven by Heather Allen, Asheville, North Carolina, from recycled fabric on cotton warp. The images were painted with fiber-reactive dyes and the design further defined with silk screen patterns. Reversible. *Photo by John Lucas.*

Plate 3. Kentucky Mountain Rug (Project 10) woven by Janet Meany. Large block units of Log Cabin are used as a border design on this rug. The colors are reversed on the other side. *Photo by Nancy Leeper.*

Plate 4. Tapestry Weave Runner, weaver unknown, collection of the American Swedish Institute, Minneapolis, Minnesota. Shown in its traditional use surrounding a table for a festive occasion. *Photo by Phyllis Waggoner.*

Plate 5. Detail, Rainbow Stripe Rug woven by Helga Johnson, Two Harbors, Minnesota. Rags were dyed in a color gradation for this rug. *Photo by Nancy Leeper.*

Plate 6. Sock Top Bath Mat (Project 1) woven by Paula Pfaff. Weft of sock top "loopers" arranged in hit-and-miss style makes a luxuriously thick rug. *Photo by Nancy Leeper.*

Plate 7. Diamond Tube Rug (Project 3) woven by Donna Sovick. Five colors of fabric were sewn into a large tube, cut, and woven in hit-and-miss fashion. *Photo by Phyllis Waggoner.*

Plate 8. Log Cabin Rug with Side Border Stripes (Project 7) woven by Helga Johnson, Two Harbors, Minnesota. The block design was created with two wefts of contrasting color. *Photo by Nancy Leeper.*

Plate 9. The Hollywood Rug (Project 16), featured in an instruction booklet from The Newcomb Loom Company, ca. 1930. This pattern was often threaded on new factory-built looms. *Photo by Phyllis Waggoner.*

Plate 10. Rep Weave Rug (Project 6) by an unknown weaver. This Log Cabin rug in heavy carpet warp was purchased in an Amish community. *Collection of Susan Barker. Photo by Phyllis Waggoner.*

Plate 11. Red, White, and Blue Log Cabin Rug (Project 9) woven by Janet Meany. Recycled denim creates this lively block-design rug. *Photo by Nancy Leeper.*

Plate 12. Room-Sized Rag Rug (Project 20) woven by Paula Pfaff. This carpet was custom-woven for the McKay farmhouse, Hudson, Wisconsin, using wool fabrics in hit-and-miss pattern on a polyester warp. Rag rug strips were lashed together to form the carpet. *Photo by Karen Searle.*

Plate 13. Detail of Ruby in Paradise, woven by Johanna Erickson, Watertown, Massachusetts. Bold asymmetrical Log Cabin design done with new cotton fabrics on cotton warp. *Photo by Joel Weisberg.*

Plate 14. Detail of Weft-Faced Twill Rug woven by Jan Nylander, Minneapolis, Minnesota. Cotton strips, cut one-half inch wide, are woven on heavy cotton warp set at 5 ends per inch. *Photo by Nancy Bundt.*

Plate 15. Shaft Switched Rug woven by Mary Anne Wise, Stockholm, Wisconsin. Hand-dyed, recycled cotton bed sheets woven on linen warp. *Photo by Peter Lee.*

2

4

5

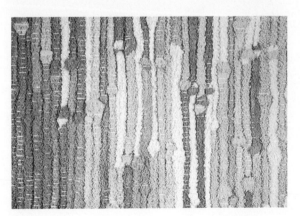

6

7

8

9

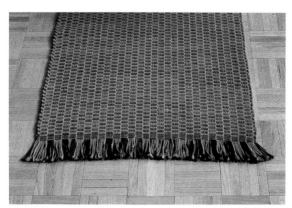

10

11

12

13

14

15

Project 1: Sock Top Bathmat

Hit-and-Miss

Cotton sock tops are a novel weft material. They produce a thick, fluffy rug or bath mat.

- **Warp.** 8/4 cotton carpet warp.
- **Weft.** 4 pounds cotton sock tops, commonly called "loopers".
- **Sett.** 10 e.p.i. See hint below.
- **Width in reed.** 30".
- **Total number of warp ends.** 300.
- **Threading.** 1,2,1,2. See draft in figure 4-6.

Preparing the weft

Chain the sock tops together. Pull on the loops when chaining so that the knots will flatten out as much as possible. By adding texture to the weaving, the knots become a prominent part of the rug's design.

A chain of 20 to 25 loops is easy to handle and long enough to fill a rug shuttle. If colored loopers are used, the weft chains can be joined to form either stripes or a random color pattern. A sett of 10 e.p.i. makes a fairly thick rug.

Weaving

1. Weave a heading with carpet warp doubled.
2. Weave body with sock top wefts, changing colors at random until desired rug length.
3. Finish with a similar heading.

> ### HINT
> *Any sett from 6 to 10 e.p.i. can be used for this rug. The thickness of the rug and the amount of weft material needed increase with the wider setts.*

Source: "Sock Top Bathmat" by Paula Pfaff in *The Weaver's Journal*, Vol. X, No. 4, Spring 1986.

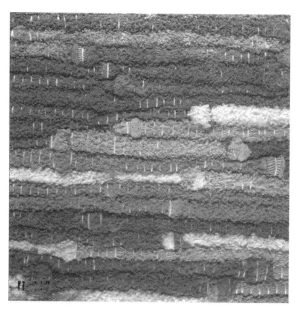

Detail, Sock Top Bathmat, woven by Paula Pfaff.

A

B

C

Chaining the sock tops. A) Lay loop 2 on top of loop 1. B) Bring the end of loop 2 through loop 1. C) Pull on loops so knot tightens.

Detail, Tube Rug, woven by Paula Pfaff.

I use Fray Check or diluted white glue along the first two rows and last two rows of the heading. This holds it in place and makes knotting go much faster. I also need fewer rows of filler.

Lorraine Goodlad
New Richmond, Wisconsin

Project 2: Tube Rug
Hit-and-Miss

One of the quickest ways to prepare rags for a rug is to sew large pieces of fabric into a tube and cut the tube into a continuous strip. *See Chapter Two, figure 2-2.* Then the fun begins. If you weave the strip in the same order in which the segments are sewn, geometric designs will appear in the rug, as if by magic. This happens because the colored segments are all the same length and appear in the same sequence.

To make the geometric effect as obvious as possible, construct the tube so that the length of each colored segment is just a bit longer than the width of the rug.

- **Warp.** 8/4 cotton carpet warp.
- **Weft.** Cotton or cotton-polyester T-shirt knit fabric, 30–60" wide; four pieces, one yard each in white, yellow, green, blue.
- **Sett.** 12 e.p.i.
- **Width in reed.** 28".
- **Total number of warp ends.** 336.
- **Threading.** 1,2,1,2. See draft in figure 4-6.

Preparing the Rags

1. Take four pieces of knit fabric, white, yellow, green, and blue and sew them together (selvedge to selvedge) to make a giant tube.

2. Fold tube so it overlaps to within 6" of top seam. The juncture of the blue and white fabrics will form the top seam. Other seams will fall at random. The piece will be very large, so work on the floor or at a large table.

3. Cut 4" strips. Starting at the bottom, work up toward the top fold. Cut through the first fold (A) but stop cutting 6" below the top seam. Cut the entire piece in this manner. The strips do not have to be exactly 4" wide. Variations of up to one inch will not be noticeable after weaving.

4. Slide your arm through the tube along the top blue-and-white seam as though it were a sleeve and cut from the first cut (A) to the selvedge to make the end of the strip. Let this strip fall to floor.

5. Make the next cut (B) diagonally from the second cut on the white side to the first cut on blue side. Continue making diagonal cuts all the way across the tube.

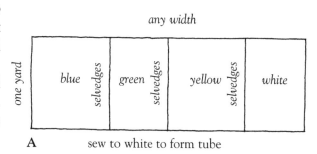

Weaving

1. Weave a heading with carpet warp doubled.

2. Wind shuttles with the tube strips. Start with blue end, strip M. Fill the shuttle to end with a white strip. Start each shuttle with blue and end with white.

3. Weave in tabby weave. The colors will appear in a pattern determined by their length. Short pieces of color will zigzag across the rug.

4. Repeat heading.

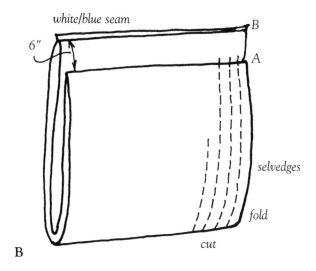

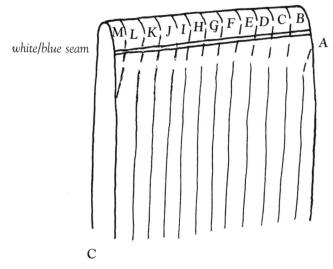

Tube preparation. A) Seam four pieces of fabric together. Sew blue end to white end to form a large tube. B) Fold tube end A to within 6 inches of top B. Slit tube through all thicknesses stopping just past edge A. C) Connect the slits by slipping your arm under uncut section of tube. Make end cut A, then make cut B across seam. Continue cutting across to M. Begin winding the shuttle with end M.

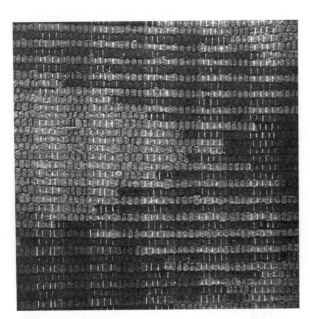

Detail, Diamond Rug, woven by Donna Sovick.

56½"

dark	medium	light	medium dark	medium light

Color arrangement for tube.

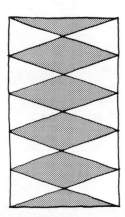

Diamond design.

Project 3: Diamond Rug

Hit-and-Miss

This carefully patterned rug is a version of the Tube Rug in *Project 2*.

- **Warp.** 8/4 cotton carpet warp arranged in stripe sequence of 8 natural, 2 gray, 8 black. Repeat 13 times.
- **Weft.** Felted wool coat-weight fabric in five shades of the same color.
- **Sett.** 8 e.p.i.
- **Width in reed.** 29 1/4".
- **Total number of warp ends.** 234.
- **Threading.** 1,2,1,2. See draft in figure 4-6.

Preparing the Rags

1. Arrange the five shades of wool in this sequence: dark, medium, light, medium dark, medium light. The pieces should be about the same size and, when pieced together, have a width of 56½" flat.

2. Sew the wool pieces together using a zigzag stitch. A) Lay two colors side-by-side at the sewing machine. B) Butt the edges closely together and zigzag flat. Be sure to feed the fabric evenly so that the pieces will lie flat.

3. Sew into a tube and cut in 1/2" strips. See *Project 2* for cutting instructions.

Weaving

1. Weave a heading with carpet warp doubled.

2. Wind shuttles starting always with a dark strip and ending with a medium-light strip. Several sequences of shades can be wound on the same shuttle.

3. Weave in tabby weave, always maintaining the shade sequence until the desired length and pattern evolves.

4. Repeat heading.

Designed by Donna Sovick.

Project 4: Checkerboard Rug

Plaid

The checkerboard rug is woven with two colors in the warp and two colors in the weft.

- **Warp.** 8/4 cotton carpet warp in black and white.
- **Weft.** Fabric strips in two colors, light and dark.
- **Sett.** 12 e.p.i.
- **Width in reed.** 28".
- **Total number of warp ends.** 336.
- **Threading.** 1,2,1,2. See draft in figure 4-6.
- **Warp color sequence.** Use 12 ends black and 12 ends white in alternate sections.

Weaving

1. Weave a heading with carpet warp doubled.
2. Using fabric strips, weave 1" with light colors, 1" with dark.
3. Continue for desired length. The checkerboard pattern will appear.
4. Repeat heading.

Source: *Instructions and Designs for the Universal Four Harness Loom.* The Deen Loom Company, Harlan, Iowa, ca. 1910.

Detail, Checkerboard Rug, woven by Janet Meany.

HINT
Always use an uneven number of shots for one of the colors so that color changes at the selvedges alternate sides.

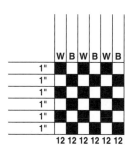

Detail, Log Cabin Rug, woven by Mitsuko Shaw.

Project 5: Basic Log Cabin Rug

Log Cabin

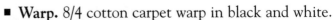

The Log Cabin pattern is called *Honeycomb* in some old instruction books. It is not to be confused with the four-shaft weave that produces small squared "cells" resembling the honeycombs bees make.

All Log Cabin variations can be woven on a two-shaft loom, but if your loom has four shafts you can use them all by threading in a 1,2,3,4 sequence. Two colors of cotton carpet warp alternate and the order of the colors changes after each group of 12 ends. A single color fabric can be used for the weft. See page 39 for more information on the Log Cabin weave.

When winding warp for Log Cabin, use either two spools (one black, one white) or four spools (two black and two white). Wind the ends together on the warping board or reel. In the threading, the black and white ends alternate, except at the boundaries between groups of 12 ends, in which two black or two white ends are next to each other. When threading, select the appropriate color from the cross.

- **Warp.** 8/4 cotton carpet warp in black and white.
- **Weft.** Fabric strips in one color.
- **Sett.** 12 e.p.i.
- **Width in reed.** 28".
- **Total number of warp ends.** 336 (168 black, 168 white).
- **Threading.** 1,2,1,2 (or 1,2,3,4,1,2,3,4). See threading at right.

Weaving

1. Weave heading with carpet warp doubled.
2. Weave rug with one shuttle wound with fabric strips sewn together.
3. Repeat heading.

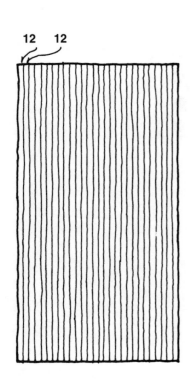

12   12

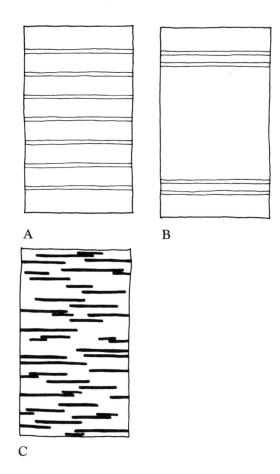

VARIATIONS

Try the following to add weft interest to the basic Log Cabin threading.

1. Insert a contrasting weft stripe at regular intervals.

2. Place one or two border stripes at each end of the rug.

3. Hit-and-Miss with Log Cabin. Use four or five different weft fabrics, weaving them in the same sequence throughout the rug, ending and beginning anywhere in the row. Each color fabric strip should extend for no more than two or three rows, or a definite stripe pattern will emerge.

Source: *Newcomb Loom Instruction Book.* The Newcomb Loom Co., Davenport, Iowa. This manual includes directions for sectional warping of the Log Cabin pattern. See *Suppliers List* for ordering information.

Variations. A) Contrasting stripes. B) Border stripes. C) Hit-and-Miss combination.

Two-shaft Threading

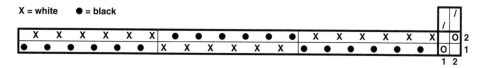

Four-shaft Threading

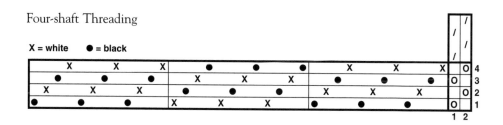

Project 6: Rep Weave Rug

Log Cabin

The warp, which is thick and closely set, provides the color interest in this rug.

- **Warp.** 4/4 cotton carpet warp in black, medium blue, dark blue.
- **Weft.** Fabric strips, all one shade of blue.
- **Sett.** 15 e.p.i.
- **Width in reed.** 28⅔".
- **Total number of warp ends.** 430.
- **Threading.** 1,2,1,2. See diagram for color order.

Weaving

1. Weave 6 shots of black 4/4 cotton carpet warp to form heading.
2. Weave entire rug with blue fabric strips.
3. Repeat heading.
4. To finish fringe, machine stitch on the last row of each heading. Knotting is unnecessary because the warp is so closely set.

4/4 carpet warp is available from Edgemont Yarn Service. See *Suppliers List* for ordering information.

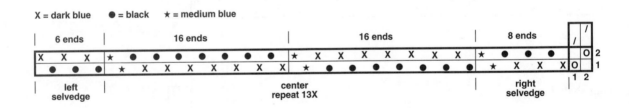

Detail, Rep Weave Rug, weaver unknown, collection of Susan Barker.

Project 7: Rug with Side Border Stripes
Log Cabin

This rug combines the basic Log Cabin weave with warp stripes on the sides. Two contrasting wefts used alternately create a block design.

- **Warp.** 8/4 cotton carpet warp in four colors: red, orange, black, white.
- **Weft.** Fabric strips in two colors: one dark, one light.
- **Sett.** 10 e.p.i.
- **Width in reed.** 30⅓".
- **Total number of warp ends.** 304.
- **Threading.** 1,2,1,2. See diagram for color order.

Weaving

1. Weave heading using carpet warp doubled.
2. Wind two shuttles, one with dark fabric, the other with light. See page 22 for weaving with two shuttles.
3. Weave in one of the three following ways:
   A) Weave 2 dark or 2 light shots at block change: 8 shots light and dark alternating for each block.
   B) Weave 2 light shots at block change:
      8 shots dark and light alternating;
      1 shot light;
      8 shots dark and light alternating;
      1 shot light.
   C) Hit-and-Miss style: Weave random amounts of four or five fabric colors repeated in the same sequence throughout the rug. Weave one to three shots of each before changing colors.
4. Repeat heading.

Designed by Helga Johnson.

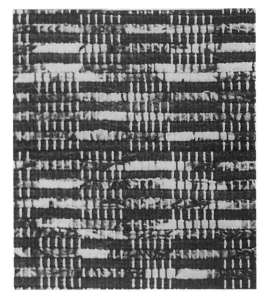

Log Cabin Rug with side stripes, woven by Helga Johnson.

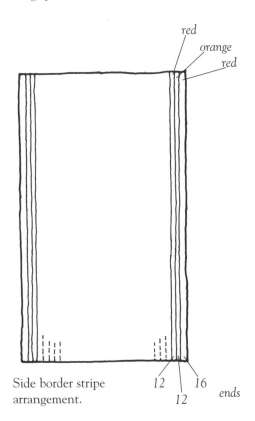

Side border stripe arrangement.

Two-shaft Threading

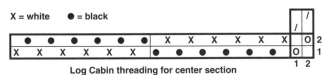

Log Cabin threading for center section

Project 8: Brick and Block Rug

Log Cabin

Details, Log Cabin block work and brick work variations, woven by Janet Meany.

brick work   **block work**

12 12 12 12   12 12 12 12
ends   ends

Warp color arrangement. Use threading in *Project 7*.

A further development of the Log Cabin weave is the addition of another weft, usually 8/4 carpet warp. This alternates with the rag strips to create distinct blocks of color. A dark square appears where black warp ends cover the rag strip, and a light area appears where white ends cover it. You may design squares (blocks) or oblong shapes (bricks) with this weave.

Weaving the blocks to "square" is referred to as "block work" in The Newcomb Loom Co. Instruction Book. The term "brick work" is used to describe the same design with narrower, brick-shaped blocks.

- **Warp.** 8/4 cotton carpet warp in two colors: black and white.
- **Weft.** Fabric strips and 8/4 carpet warp (black or white).
- **Sett.** 12 e.p.i.
- **Width in reed.** 28".
- **Total number of warp ends.** 336.
- **Threading.** 1,2,1,2. See diagram for color order.

Weaving

The main part of the rug is woven with two shuttles. See two-shuttle weaving, page 22. Wind one shuttle with fabric strips, the other with carpet warp.

1. Weave a heading with carpet warp doubled.
2. Alternate one shot of fabric with one shot of carpet warp until a square is formed. The block can be changed by weaving two consecutive shots of fabric or two consecutive shots of warp.
3. Continue with alternate shots of warp and fabric until another block is formed. Weave for desired length.
4. Repeat heading.

Source: *Instruction Book for the Newcomb Improved No. 3 Loom.* The Newcomb Loom Co., Davenport, Iowa.

Project 9: Large Red, White, and Blue Rug

Log Cabin

Recycled denim is a popular filler for rugs. When woven with this Log Cabin threading, the light and dark squares bordered with red make a lively rug. Because denim is heavy and hard to beat into place, cut strips no wider than 1" to 1½" in width. If your strips are thinner than this, you may need to weave more than six shots to square the block.

- **Warp.** 8/4 cotton carpet warp in red, white, and black.
- **Weft.** Blue denim and black (or white or red) carpet warp.
- **Sett.** 12 e.p.i.
- **Width in reed.** 28⅓".
- **Total number of warp ends.** 340.
- **Threading.** 1,2,1,2. See draft below.

Detail, Denim Log Cabin Rug, woven by Janet Meany.

Weaving

Wind two shuttles, one with denim, the other with carpet warp. See page 22 for weaving with two shuttles.

1. Weave a heading with carpet warp doubled.

2. Weave alternate shots with the two shuttles until the block is squared. Six shots of denim and six shots of carpet warp will usually make a square.

3. Weave one more shot of carpet warp to change the block.

4. Weave the next square. Weave the main body of the rug.

5. Weave a heading.

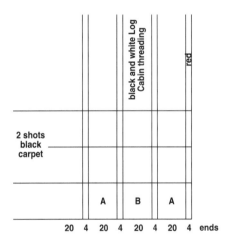

Color arrangement.

Source: Tod and Del Deo, *Designing and Making Handwoven Rugs.* 1976, page 94.

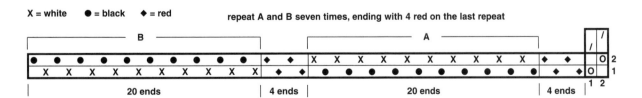

Project 10: Kentucky Mountain Pattern Rug

Log Cabin

Detail, Kentucky Mountain Pattern Rug, woven by Janet Meany.

The Log Cabin weave is not restricted to blocks and bricks. Any size blocks can be created. The Kentucky Mountain pattern consists of a large center block bordered with smaller blocks, and produces a rug that is predominantly light on one side and dark on the other.

- **Warp.** 8/4 cotton carpet warp in black and white.
- **Weft.** Fabric strips, one color; carpet warp, black or white.
- **Sett.** 12 e.p.i.
- **Width in reed.** 28".
- **Total number of warp ends.** 335.
- **Threading.** 1,2,1,2. See draft at right.

WARPING HINT
When threading the pattern, check at the beginning of each section to see that the correct color warp is on the correct shaft.

Reverse side of Kentucky Mountain Rug.

Weaving

Wind two shuttles, one with fabric strips, the other with a single strand of carpet warp. See page 22 for weaving with two shuttles.

1. Weave a heading with carpet warp doubled.

2. Weave 5½" alternating fabric strips and carpet warp.

3. Shift the block by weaving two shots of carpet warp.

4. Continue alternating fabric and warp until a 1" area is squared.

5. Weave two shots of carpet warp to change the block.

6. Continue weaving blocks as shown in the diagram.

7. Repeat heading.

Source: Alice K. Cripps, *Adventures in Weaving on a 2 Harness Loom.*

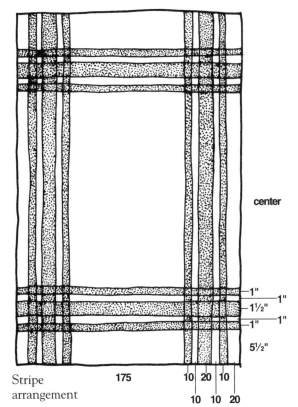

center

1"
1"
1½"
1"
1"
5½"

Stripe arrangement

175   10 20 10
       10 10 20

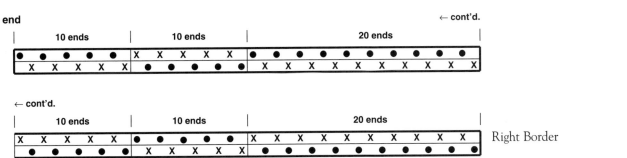

end   ← cont'd.

| 10 ends | 10 ends | 20 ends |

← cont'd.

| 10 ends | 10 ends | 20 ends | Right Border

● = black
X = white

175 ends

end center section here   Center

begin and end with black

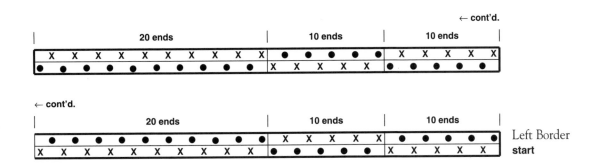

                                                    ← cont'd.

| 20 ends | 10 ends | 10 ends |

← cont'd.

| 20 ends | 10 ends | 10 ends | Left Border
                                    start

Detail, Log Cabin Rug with block border, woven by Ruby Jansen.

Project 11: Block Border Rug
Log Cabin

This variation combines side warp stripes with a center area of Log Cabin and a block border at each end. For the body of the rug, three or four fabrics can be used in sequence in Hit-and-Miss fashion. The borders are done with two shuttles, one with rag weft and the other with carpet warp. These are alternated to produce the border design.

- **Warp.** 8/4 cotton carpet warp in black and white.
- **Weft.** Fabric strips in three or four coordinated colors; carpet warp for borders.
- **Sett.** 12 e.p.i.
- **Width in reed.** 28".
- **Total number of warp ends.** 336.
- **Threading.** 1,2,1,2. See diagram and color sequence at right.

Warp Color Sequence

48 black and white alternating (border threading)
6 black solid stripe
12 white solid stripe
6 black solid stripe
192 black and white alternating in 8 groups of 24
   (Log Cabin threading)
6 black solid stripe
12 white solid stripe
6 black solid stripe
48 black and white alternating (border threading)

> *WARPING HINT*
> *When you start threading the last 48-end black-and-white stripe, be sure to thread all the black ends on the same shaft or shafts they were threaded on in the first 48-end stripe. If the black ends are on shaft 1 (or 1 and 3) in the first stripe, place them on shaft 1 (or 1 and 3) in the last stripe. Start the last 48 ends with a black end even though the previous 6 ends are black.*

I started to weave when I was 10 or 11 years old. I used to help my aunt from Sweden string up the loom. We'd set it up in an outbuilding on the farm. We threaded a pattern she had learned in Sweden. Border: 14 brown, 12 tan, 12 mixed brown-tan [Log Cabin], 12 tan, 12 brown. Center: groups of 12 mixed brown-tan [Log Cabin]. Border: 12 brown, 12 tan, 12 mixed, 12 tan, 14 brown.

Margaret Sande
Two Harbors, Minnesota

Weaving

1. Weave a heading with carpet warp doubled.

2. Weave no more than two or three rows of each color fabric in sequence, Hit-and-Miss fashion (see *Project 1*). If you want definite stripes, begin and end each color at the selvedges.

3. Border Pattern.
    A) Begin the rug with 4½" of the colored fabrics woven in sequence.
    B) Border rows:
        2 shots of rag color A
        1 shot rag color B
        1 shot of black carpet warp
        2 shots of rag color B
        1 shot black carpet warp
        2 shots rag color B
        1 shot black carpet warp
        1 shot rag color B
        2 shots of rag color A

4. Continue weaving with the sequence of colored fabric strips in the center section (about 26").

5. Weave the second border following the sequence above.

6. Complete rug with 4½" of the sequence of colored fabric strips.

7. Repeat heading.

Designed by Ruby Jansen.

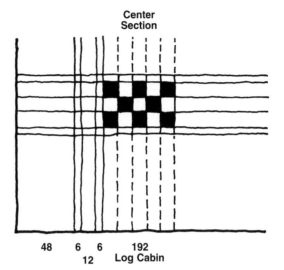

Center
Section

48   6   6   192
    12   Log Cabin

Block Arrangement.

Log Cabin

X = white   ● = black

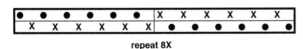

repeat 8X

63

Project 12: Mixed Stripe Rug

Log Cabin and Plain

There are endless possibilities for Log Cabin variations. This rug is a combination of solid colored and Log Cabin patterned stripes. These are separated by narrow bands of a third color.

- **Warp.** 8/4 cotton carpet warp in three colors: black, white, red.
- **Weft.** Fabric strips, Hit-and-Miss or a single color.
- **Sett.** 12 e.p.i.
- **Width in reed.** 29".
- **Total number of warp ends.** 352.
- **Threading.** See draft and diagram below.

Weaving

1. Weave a heading with carpet warp doubled.
2. There are two ways to weave this rug:
   A) Weave a Hit-and-Miss pattern using one shuttle. See *Project 1*.
   B) Weave a ribbed pattern with two shuttles: one with fabric strips, the other with carpet warp. Dark and light blocks will form in the Log Cabin stripe areas. See *Ribbed Weave*, page 34.

Source: *Deen Loom Instruction Book*, The Deen Loom Company, Harlan, Iowa.

Detail, Mixed Stripe Rug, woven by Paula Pfaff.

Log Cabin threading for black-and-white stripe

X = white　　● = black

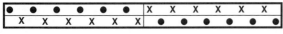

repeat 2X

Warp Color Arrangement.

8	48	6	36	6	48	6	36	6	48	6	36	6	48	8
white	black and white Log Cabin	white	red	white	black and white Log Cabin	white	red	white	black and white Log Cabin	white	red	white	black and white Log Cabin	white

Project 13: Basic Twill Rug
Twill

Twill patterns have always been popular with rag rug weavers because customers like the look of a "fancy" weave. The ability to produce twills was a strong selling point for the factory-built four-shaft fly-shuttle looms such as those made by the Deen and Newcomb companies.

Some weavers feel that twill rugs do not wear as well as tabby because the twill warp, not the filling, gets the wear. You will find that you can weave a firm, tightly constructed rug in twill if you experiment with the sett and thickness of the strips.

- **Warp.** 8/4 cotton carpet warp: colored stripes or all one color. Experiment with various combinations of colors in the warp stripes.
- **Weft.** Fabric strips, solid or figured.
- **Sett.** 10 e.p.i.
- **Width in reed.** 30".
- **Total number of warp ends.** 300.
- **Threading.** 1,2,3,4. See draft below and on page 66, or use any twill pattern.

Weaving

1. Weave a heading in tabby or twill using carpet warp doubled.

2. For the body of the rug, experiment with the thickness of the rag strips. Use slightly thinner rags for a dense weave. Wider rags make a thick rug with long floats of warp (less durable).

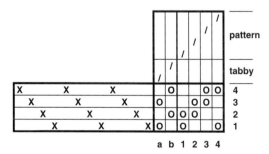

Project draft: standard twill.

—*continued on page 66*

Detail, Twill Rug, woven by Paula Pfaff.

Additional Twill Threading Drafts.

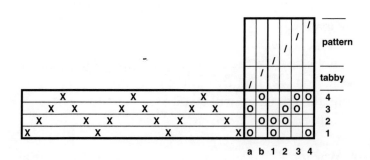

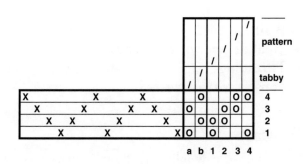

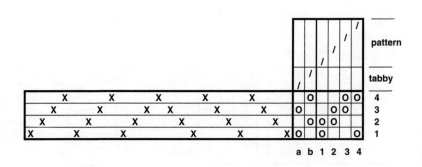

Project 14: Anderson Weave Rug

Twill

Instructions for producing the "Anderson Rug" on the *Weaver's Delight Four Harness Loom* were offered to Newcomb Loom customers in an instruction manual published in the early twentieth century. According to the manual, "It is a very attractive design and should prove a ready seller." The threading is four-shaft twill.

When winding warp, use two spools of carpet warp (one black, one white). Wind the ends together on a warping board or reel. Wind four extra white ends.

- **Warp.** 8/4 cotton carpet warp in black and white.
- **Weft.** Fabric strips in light green, brown, tan.
- **Sett.** 12 e.p.i.
- **Width in reed.** 28⅓".
- **Total number of warp ends.** 340.
- **Threading.** See draft on next page.

Detail, Anderson Weave Rug, woven by Paula Pfaff.

Weaving

1. Weave a heading in either tabby or twill with carpet warp doubled.

2. Begin the rug with light green, following the twill treadling shown in the draft. Start weft at left side to include all warp ends in the selvedge.

3. Color sequence for border:

5" light green
3 shots brown
7 shots tan
3 shots brown
7 shots light green
3 shots brown
7 shots tan
3 shots brown

—*continued on page 68*

4. Weave 37" light green.

5. Second border: repeat sequence above in reverse order, finishing with 5" of light green.

6. Weave heading.

Source: *Instructions for The Weaver's Delight Four Harness, Fly Shuttle Loom*, The Newcomb Loom Co., Davenport, Iowa. This manual includes directions for sectional warping of the Anderson weave and other patterns. See *Suppliers List* for ordering information.

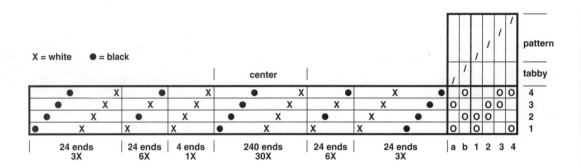

X = white   ● = black

			pattern / tabby
● X ● X	● X ● X	● X ● X ●	O . . O O	4
● X X X	● X X X	● X X ●	O . O O .	3
● X ● X	● X ● X	● X ● ●	O O O . .	2
● X X X	● X X X	● X X ●	O . O . O	1
24 ends 3X	24 ends 6X · 4 ends 1X	240 ends 30X · 24 ends 6X · 24 ends 3X	a b 1 2 3 4	

center

Anderson Weave Rug.

Project 15: Double Seed Rug
Twill

This popular old rug design has been described as "chicken tracks" because of the pattern formed by the sets of three colored ends in the warp. You need a four-shaft loom to weave this rug.

- **Warp.** 8/4 cotton carpet warp in black and white.
- **Weft.** Fabric strips in one color or a sequence of colors.
- **Sett.** 12 e.p.i.
- **Width in reed.** 27".
- **Total number of warp ends.** 324.
- **Threading.** Black: 1,2,1; white 4,3,4. See draft below.

Weaving

1. Weave a heading in tabby weave with carpet warp doubled.

2. Weave the main body of the rug following the treadling order in the draft. If the loom has only four treadles, use a direct tie-up (see figure 4-4 on page 43).

Source: Plath, Iona. *The Craft of Handweaving.* New York: Charles Scribner's Sons, 1972, page 89.

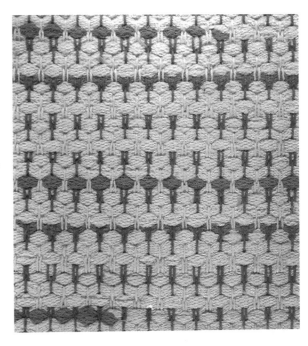

Detail, Double Seed Rug, woven by Mary Cook.

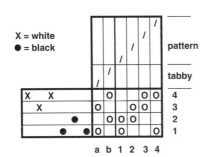

Detail, Hollywood Rug, weaver unknown, collection of Susan Barker.

Project 16: The Hollywood Rug
Twill

The *Hollywood Weave* was included in The Newcomb Loom Company's instruction manual. In fact, the enduring pattern was threaded on the looms before they left the factory. Hollywood combines elements of the Double Seed and twill weaves.

- **Warp.** 8/4 cotton carpet warp in black and white.
- **Weft.** Fabric strips in tan, white, brown.
- **Sett.** 12 e.p.i.
- **Width in reed.** 28".
- **Total number of warp ends.** 335.
- **Threading.** See draft at right.

Weaving

1. Weave a heading in tabby or twill with carpet warp doubled.
2. Follow the twill treadling shown in the draft.
3. Border sequence:
   5" tan (40 shots of rug filler)
   1 shot white
   5 shots brown
   1 shot white
   25 shots light blue
   1 shot white
   5 shots brown
   1 shot white

These instructions are for weaving with rug filler. If you are using rags, reduce the number of shots in each color area.

4. Weave 35" tan.
5. Second border: repeat above sequence in reverse order, finishing with 5" of tan.
6. Repeat heading.

Source: *Instructions for The Weaver's Delight Four Harness, Fly Shuttle
Loom*, The Newcomb Loom Co., Davenport, Iowa. This manual and the
Instruction Book for the Studio Four Harness Art Loom contain directions
for sectional warping of this pattern and others. See *Suppliers List* for
ordering information.

Cut the bread wrapper lengthwise.
Open it out and lay [it] in the shed. I cut
the ends narrower where you join the pieces.
The rugs are made from the wrappers from
cracked wheat bread. We ate that for years and
that's what I got out of it—a rug!

Esther Kyromaki
Duluth, Minnesota

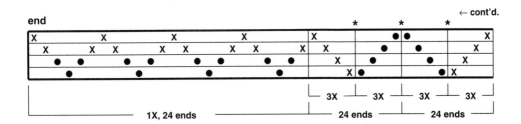

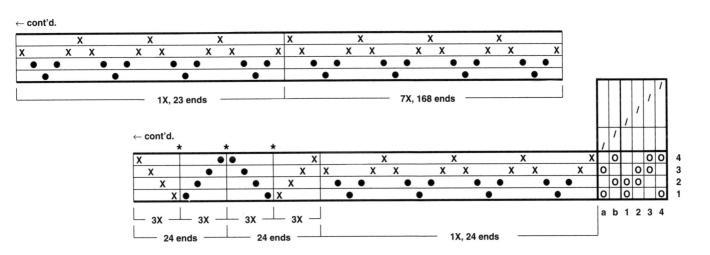

X = white   ● = black   *These are not mistakes. The two ends are on the same shaft, but not in the same heddle or in the same dent.

Project 17: Reversible Weave Rug

Twill

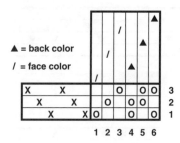

Detail, Reversible Weave Rug, woven by Paula Pfaff.

This is an exciting rug to weave! You can place bright colors on one side and dark or neutral colors on the other. Both sides of the rug have a twill design.

- **Warp.** 8/4 cotton carpet warp.
- **Weft.** Fabric strips.
- **Sett.** 6 doubled e.p.i. (for a 12-dent reed, sley every other dent).
- **Width in reed.** 30".
- **Total number of warp ends.** 360 (180 working ends).
- **Threading.** 1,2,3,1,2,3. See draft below.

Weaving

Use a direct tie-up if your loom has only four treadles (see figure 4-6 on page 43). There is no tabby weave in this threading.

1. Weave a heading with carpet warp doubled. Use the treadling sequence for the body.

2. For the body, use two shuttles with contrasting rag strips and follow the treadling sequence. Start one shuttle from each side. Weave for desired length.

3. Repeat heading.

Source: Rogers, Carrie M. "The Story of My Dining Room Rug" in *The Weaver's Journal*, Vol. 6, No. 4. Spring 1982. To weave this rug on a two-shaft loom, see "Reversible Rug" designed by Jery Oles in *Just Rags*, Interweave Press, 1985. Also see Collingwood, pages 279–280.

3 shafts, 6 treadles

▲ = back color

/ = face color

X		X		O		O O	3
	X		X	O	O O		2
		X	X O		O	O	1

1 2 3 4 5 6

Project 18: Double Binding Rug

Twill

This Swedish design produces a reversible rug with a block pattern. Rag strips should be narrow and firmly packed to cover the underlying warp ends.

- **Warp.** 8/4 cotton carpet warp.
- **Weft.** Fabric strips, 1/2" wide, in two or more contrasting colors.
- **Sett.** 16 e.p.i.
- **Width in reed.** 29¾".
- **Total number of warp ends.** 475.
- **Threading.** See draft and diagram below.

Weaving

1. Weave a heading in tabby. There will be *double warp ends* at the block change. This is not an error.

2. Wind two shuttles with contrasting colors. Alternate colors as you weave, following the treadling sequence in the draft. For example:

      treadle 4, weave dark weft
      treadle 3, weave light weft
      treadle 2, weave dark weft
      treadle 1, weave light weft.

3. Continue with this color sequence for 6".

4. Reverse color order:

      treadle 4, weave light weft
      treadle 3, weave dark weft, etc.

5. Continue for 6". Alternate blocks for remainder of rug.

6. Repeat heading.

W E A V I N G   H I N T S
*Beat very firmly.
*To make blocks square, weave them a little longer than square to allow for shrinkage when the rug is removed from the loom.

Source: Inga Krook, "From Rags to Riches", in *Handwoven*, Vol. 4, No. 3. Summer 1983.

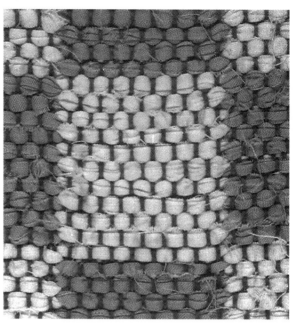

Detail, Double Binding Rug, woven by Karen Janezich.

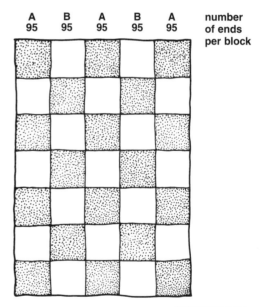

A 95	B 95	A 95	B 95	A 95	number of ends per block

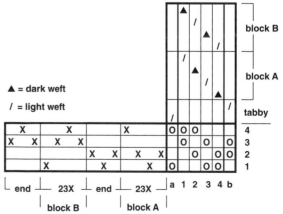

▲ = dark weft

/ = light weft

Project 19: Blocks of Color Rug
Block Weave

"Window pane" is the term often used to describe this rug. At least four shafts are required. If more shafts are available, more blocks can be made. It is woven with fabric strips in two contrasting colors. The wefts exchange surfaces. Because the warp shows, it is important that it harmonize with the wefts.

- **Warp.** 10/2 linen or 8/4 cotton carpet warp.
- **Weft.** Fabric strips in two contrasting colors.
- **Sett.** 12 e.p.i.
- **Width in reed.** 28".
- **Total number of warp ends.** 336.

Threading

See diagram below and draft on next page. The groups of three ends can be threaded in the same heddle but should be sleyed separately in the reed.

The design is divided into two blocks, Block A and Block B. Thread the blocks as indicated in the diagram.

Weaving

1. Weave a heading with carpet warp doubled. There is no true tabby with this weave. Follow the 1,2,3,4 treadling sequence shown for the body. Keep the same treadling sequence throughout the weaving.

2. Begin with background color. Weave 6½".

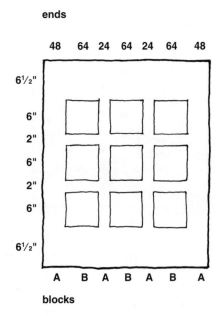

Detail, Block Weave Rug, woven by Janet Meany.

3. Start the contrasting color to form the block shapes. Weave with the two shuttles, background color in the background, block color in the blocks. Weave according to the diagram for the size of the blocks.

4. Weave a heading.

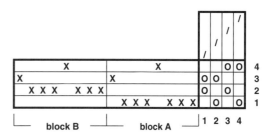

THREADING:
block A 6 times
block B 8 times
block A 3 times
block B 8 times
block A 3 times
block B 8 times
block A 6 times

WEAVING HINTS

This rug draws in a lot. Be sure to always place the weft at an angle in the shed.

The background color can be put on two shuttles. The selvedges are sometimes firmer if two shuttles are used.

Other colors may be laid into the block areas. Place the laid-in materials in the same shed as the regular weft.

Beat firmly after both shuttles have been used.

Source: This threading is adapted from a project woven in a workshop taught by Ken Weaver.

Blocks of Color rug showing knotted linen warp fringe.

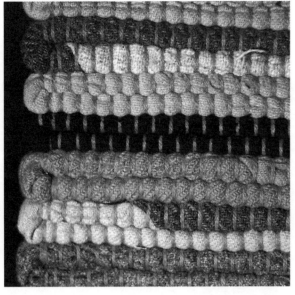

Detail, Room-sized Rag Rug, woven in three strips by Paula Pfaff.

Project 20: Room-Sized Rug
Hit-and-Miss

Historically, "rag carpets" were sold by the yard to carpet the front room or parlor. Long rug strips were laid side by side and sewn together to create the carpet. They were tacked or nailed along the walls and often were padded with fresh straw.

This rug is a variation on old carpets. The directions are for a 6'-by-9' area rug with bound ends woven in a Hit-and-Miss pattern. Two strips 36" wide and 9 feet long are lashed together to create the 6'-by-9' size. If a 40" loom is not available, make three 24" strips. A larger rug can be made by adding more strips.

The best quality carpets are made from wool fabric because it resists soiling. Old or new fabric may be used. Skirt-weight fabric is cut about 2" wide; heavy coat fabric may be cut as narrow as 1".

- **Warp.** 8/4 cotton carpet warp doubled in a 10-yard warp.
- **Weft.** 20 lb. of wool fabric in desired colors.
- **Sett.** 6 doubled e.p.i. (Two ends used as one for added strength).
- **Width in reed.** 39".
- **Total number of warp threads.** 234 pairs (468 individual ends).
- **Threading.** 1,2,3,4,1,2,3,4.

Preparing the Rags

Cut fabric into strips of assorted lengths from 8" to 45" long. Reserve 1/2 yard of one color fabric for the binding.

1. Arrange strips in equal piles by color groupings. For example: blues, greens, browns, beiges, grays. Adjust piles to approximately equal amounts. For example, if the blue pile is twice as big as the others, make a light blue pile and a dark blue pile, or combine plaids, etc.

2. Assemble a pack of variegated colors by taking one piece from each pile in a set sequence such as: one light blue, one brown, one green, one dark blue, one plaid, etc., and repeat until you have 12 to 14 pieces in each pack.

3. Take this pack to the sewing machine and sew the strips together using the bias method described in *Chapter Two*.

4. Test the pack by winding it on your shuttle. One pack should be just enough to fill it.

5. Continue making packs until all the strips are used. Packs can be tied together or stacked.

Weaving

1. Weave 3" to 4" with very fuzzy scraps to spread the warp and hold wool strips in place before knotting.

2. Begin weaving. There is no woven heading. The warp ends will be knotted and enclosed in a binding.

   A) *Beat very firmly,* allowing ample weft to prevent excessive drawing-in.

   B) Fold in the raw edges at the joins and selvedges.

   C) *Measure very carefully as you weave, without releasing tension.*

3. For a 9-foot strip, weave approximately 10 feet 2 inches, which allows $1^1/_2$" per foot for shrinkage.

4. Add 3" to 4" of filler at the end and cut the strip off the loom. Handle gently, being careful not to dislodge filler. Store loosely folded.

5. Retie warp and weave second strip, remembering to use 3" to 4" of fuzzy filler at each end.

Joining Rug Strips. Allow both strips to "relax" for several days before sewing them together. Cover the floor of your work space with a plastic drop cloth. This keeps the rug clean and allows the strips to slide and assume their "natural" length.

1. Using a sewing machine, stitch across one end of each strip on top of the last wool weft.

2. Gently remove filler at this end and knot the warps in one-inch bunches using an overhand knot.

3. Line up the strips side-by-side and measure down the *center* of each strip. (Selvedges are sometimes stretched and do not give accurate measurements.) The strips are usually not exactly the same length.

4. Mark each strip at one-foot intervals with a safety pin in the middle of the width.

5. Lash strips together through the selvedge loops using doubled cotton carpet warp and a heavy needle. The strips should match at each safety pin marker. It may be necessary to lash through two selvedge loops occasionally to keep the pieces even.

—continued on page 78

Hit-and-Miss living-room rag rug assembled from three woven strips.

I have only had my loom since 1937, but have made a good many rugs, hall runners and stair runners from 27 inches wide to 36 inch for very old houses with the old-fashioned wide stairs, most of those with hit-and-miss wool. I cut all the rags and had to wash them. I use Tide and don't rinse it all out and the moths won't ever bother them.

Mrs. Emma E. Cook, New York
The Shuttle, 1963

Project 20 continued

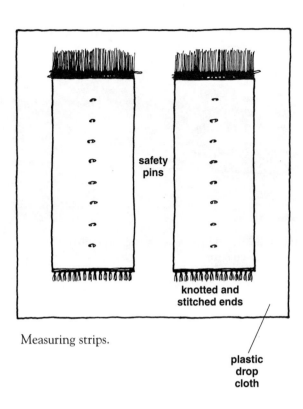

Measuring strips.

safety
pins

knotted and
stitched ends

plastic
drop
cloth

A) Insert needle in the right edge and knot thread to start.
B) Thread needle through the first loop on the left strip, then through the first loop on the right strip. Repeat, then pull hard on lashing thread. It will disappear into the flat seam.
C) Continue lashing to the end of the strips and tie off the thread.

Securing the Ends. Machine stitch across the last weft row of both strips. Knot the warp ends on one strip first, then on the second to make it match, unraveling a few rows if necessary. Trim fringe 1/2" to 1" long.

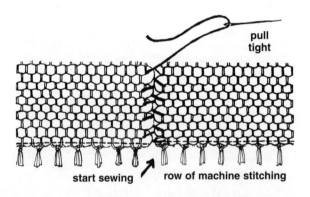

pull
tight

start sewing   row of machine stitching

Lashing strips together.

Binding. Set up your sewing machine with a table next to it to support the weight of the rug while you sew on the binding.

1. Cut the reserved 1/2 yard of fabric into 4" strips.

2. Sew the strips together with a bias join to make a strip long enough for both ends of the rug.

3. Place this binding along the top at the edge. Leave 1" free for turning in the end.

4. Sew binding to the last weft shot, stretching the binding slightly.

5. Fold binding so that edge A is tucked behind the seam, forming a double thickness.

6. Fold doubled edge over knots, tucking in ends, and zigzag-stitch on top of first row of stitching. Repeat on other end of carpet.

The rug should be installed over carpet pad cut 1" smaller on all sides.

Designed by Paula Pfaff.

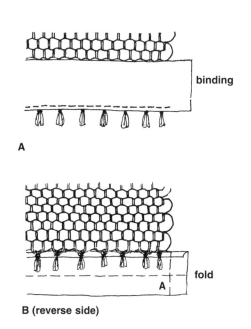

A

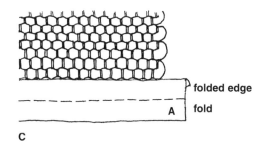

B (reverse side)

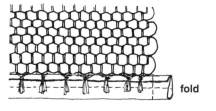

C

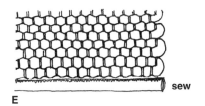

D

E

Binding the ends.

Bound edge of rag carpet.

Right. Poster from the Newcomb Loom Company, courtesy of Vesterheim, the Norwegian-American Museum, Decorah, Iowa. *Photo by Marion Nelson.*

Far right. An original water color rendering of the Newcomb Fly-Shuttle Loom. *Collection of The Newcomb Looms Historical Society.*

Chapter Five

History and Looms

My mother's cousin's husband was passing a farm one day when he saw a loom in pieces stacked against the wall. He stopped and asked if the man would sell it. The man said, 'Yes, for $5!' He had built it for his wife many years ago but she died before she could use it. My mother and as many as twelve families shared this loom. It made the rounds of all the families for 20 years. Eventually, it was burned for firewood. This is how my mother used to warp: she would put big spikes on the sides of the granary and then run around it to wind the 40 or 50 yards she needed. Somebody going by must have thought the woman was crazy!

Ina Karni
Cook, Minnesota

Rag Rug Traditions

Now that you have woven the first of many rag rugs, you may be curious about the origins of this craft and the wide variety of looms used to produce rag rugs. The history of rag weaving is largely undocumented. While it is likely that the weaving of recycled cloth dates far back into antiquity, one of the earliest known examples is a rag rug woven in eighteenth-century Japan.[1] An early documented piece of European rag weaving is a Swedish counterpane with the date 1834 woven into it. However, rag weavings were referred to before this time in old Swedish wills and estate inventories.[2] Examples of historic rag weaving from other European countries and the British Isles have been recorded in several studies.[3] Some outstanding North American examples are the *catalogne* coverlets found in Canadian museums.

Rag weaving appears to be a worldwide craft. Contemporary rag weavings are produced in Finland, Haiti, India, the former Soviet Union, and Saudi Arabia. Scandinavia's strong tradition of rug weaving is thriving in the twentieth century, and the Japanese still weave colorful *obis* (sashes), jackets, and vests with thin strips of fabric.

North American Origins

Early immigrants to the United States and Canada brought over textile tools, including spinning wheels and reeds, in their family trunks. In most cases it was not practical to bring the large floor looms required for rug weaving. Instead, looms were constructed after arrival in this country. Many early handcrafted North American rug looms are similar in design to those used in Europe at the time and were probably reconstructed from memory. Looms shown in eighteenth-century French, Dutch, British and German illustrations resemble those reproduced for weavers who emigrated from those countries.[4]

A household loom was often shared by a community, transported from farm to farm by cart and housed in an outbuilding. At least one loom in rural Minnesota was housed in a sauna. There is also evidence that looms were used in basements, attics, and kitchens.

At first, home weavers made table linens, coverlets, yardage for clothing, and other lighter weight items on their looms. Later, many four-shaft looms were con-

By the time of the Revolution, three kinds of weavers populated the colonies—home weavers, weavers who had established shops in the towns, and perhaps most interesting of all, itinerant weavers. This latter group traveled from homestead to homestead, some bringing their looms with them, others weaving on the household loom for which the farmer's wife had insufficient time, experience, or interest. With roads and communications in a rather primitive state, the itinerant weaver was always a welcome source of news and gossip. When he finally settled down, his shop became, like the country store of later times, the town center for scandal, rumors, and news.

Eric Broudy
The Book of Looms

verted to two-shaft solely for the purpose of weaving rag rugs. Women helped each other with the warping and held "rag-sewing bees" outside in the summer. Pieces of fabric from old clothes, bedspreads, curtains, blankets, sheets, etc. were cut or torn, sewn together into strips, and wound into balls.[5] Most fabrics had served out their usefulness in other capacities before they were woven into rugs. The best portions may have been reserved for quilt pattern blocks.[6] Usually only one kind of material was used for each rug, i.e., cotton rags for kitchen, bedroom, and bathroom rugs, and wool for living rooms and hallways. Silk rags were used for door curtains, scatter rugs, seat mats, and couch throws. The width of the strips varied with the type of material.

Early Patterns

"Hit-and-Miss" rugs came about because even the smallest scraps of fabric were saved and wound carefully into balls that were then woven on looms at home or taken to a local weaver to be woven. When a weaver received these balls, she had no choice but to weave them as they were sewn.[7] See figure 3-3 and *Project 1*. Later, rags of similar color were wound together to give the weaver greater latitude in designing her rugs. Stripes were sometimes made in both the warp and weft to produce a plaid effect. A *Log Cabin* pattern with dark and light threads alternating in the warp and weft was a favorite. See figure 3-18 and *Projects 5 through 12*. Twills could be woven on four-shaft looms to create an entirely different kind of surface texture and color arrangement. See *Projects 13 and 14*. In some rugs "laid in" and tufted designs were added. See figures 3-9, 3-10, and 3-11. Tapestry techniques made wedge-shaped areas possible. Sometimes two wefts were twisted together in a "turkey-track" pattern (see figure 3-7) or rags were dyed to achieve color gradations.

Each weaver had a distinctive style or trademark. For one it might be two stripes on either side of the rug; for another, it could be the insertion of bright rags to form a flower pattern in the end border stripes, or a twisted weft stripe at both ends of the weaving. This last embellishment is reminiscent of early Shaker techniques.[8] The beautiful catalogne coverlets and rugs of Canada also use a variation on the twist technique.

Early Rag Rug Use

Loom company catalogues from the early years of the twentieth century indicate that rag carpeting was used extensively in home furnishing in the United States.[9] Rag carpet strips were woven approximately 36 inches wide on looms that were 40 to 45 inches wide. These carpet strips were then joined together to cover an entire floor surface. Although warp-faced carpeting is mentioned in some early catalogs, the carpets referred to here had warp setts of 10 or 12 e.p.i. Old newsletters indicate that weaving rag rugs for carpeting or throw rugs was a profitable home occupation.[10] Many men and women were able to support themselves or supplement the family income with their weaving skills.

As floor coverings became more diverse, the rag rug was relegated to the less public rooms of the house, and carpets, domestic and imported, were used to furnish the front parlor and living room. Even the introduction of wall-to-wall carpeting has not stilled the demand for rag rugs. Begun as a necessity, rag rug weaving has endured because of the rich, warm atmosphere it creates in a home.

Illustration from *The Shuttle*, September, 1942. It accompanied an article which pointed out to members of the Maysville Guild that full-time rag rug weavers earn more than the national average wartime income: ". . . as little as a yard a day will pay the rent for a comfortable home in most small towns."

The Shuttle   September, 1942

THE DOLLAR$ and ENE of the WEAVER'S BUSINESS

Early Twentieth-Century Rug Looms

A wide variety of early handcrafted and manufactured rug looms are still in existence. The handcrafted looms described below were constructed with a minimum of woodworking tools and, in general, had few metal parts. Wedges secured the assembled pieces. The weaver depressed foot treadles to change the sheds and threw the shuttle manually. Factory-built looms described later in this section were manufactured in the late nineteenth and early twentieth centuries for the primary purpose of weaving rag rugs. They often incorporated devices utilized in commercial mechanized looms. Many were equipped with fly shuttles and used warping techniques from the textile industry. These looms were not completely automatic, however. The weaver activated the beater (and the fly shuttle) to do the weaving. Some of these looms had foot treadles. Many were constructed entirely out of metal or had many metal parts.

Handmade Looms

The opportunities for finding handmade looms are plentiful if you're willing to seek them out. Looms are frequently advertised in newspapers, farm journals, and weaving guild newsletters, or included in farm or estate sales. Often, when a farm is sold, a dismantled loom may be found in the attic, barn, or chicken house. Talking to rug weavers and antique dealers will sometimes result in information about local looms. The following descriptions of old looms will help you identify any you may find.

Handmade Counterbalanced Loom

The most common looms were made of heavy timbers similar to those used to frame a barn. The *beams* were fastened together at angles with large wooden pegs or wedges in mortise and tenon joints. The rear warp beam, often a tree trunk, had holes where a long stick or pole was inserted to adjust the tension. One antique loom we have seen still has birch bark on the beam.

Some warp beams had pegs all around with a long board between the pegs and the back post for a tensioning device. A carved wooden piece that caught the pegs on the warp beam and a weighted box suspended by a rope were other means of maintaining tension.

*F*inding that first, old loom is almost every weaver's fantasy come true—ours was occasioned by a neighbor's chance remark that maybe all those old pieces of wood upstairs of his 1820 barn were a loom. [He said it was] awfully dirty, with funny extra pieces lying around that, from his description, I knew were an umbrella swift, a warping board, and a miscellaneous bed frame. We set a date to see if it was truly a loom. Stuart and I, armed with Marion Channing's Tools of Colonial Textiles for reference, arrived eagerly at the white clapboard house, walked up [to] the front door and gasped. There on the summer porch, used as end pieces of a sturdy wooden bench and painted green, were the typical curved side pieces that hold the breast and cloth beams of nineteenth-century bench looms. Although other parts were missing, we finally managed to put together a 40-inch four-[shaft] counterbalance overhead beater barn loom.

Nan Ross
"Those Musty Old Looms",
Shuttle, Spindle & Dyepot. Spring 1977

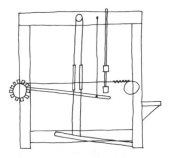

5-1. Four-Poster Loom with pole brake and built-on bench.

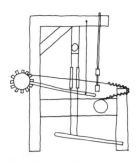

5-2. Single Rear Support Loom with angled struts.

5-3. **Loom with rear supports** cut from a single piece of wood.

The rope was tied to the loose end of the *brake* and went up over the top of the loom to the front, where the weaver could pull on it to release it. Stretched from back to front, the warp was held on the *cloth beam* and tensioned by a pawl and ratchet wheel, often a flat circular metal disk with notches. The *beater* was hung from the overhead frame; its height and position could be adjusted. The *treadles*, which raised and lowered the pattern shafts, were usually attached at the rear of the loom with long pegs. *Reeds* were made of narrow strips of marsh reeds set into a frame and bound with twine.

Warp ends were threaded through *heddles* made of linen or cotton. The heddles, either individual or all of one piece, were strung between two wooden *shaft* rods suspended from the loom frame by ropes. Pulleys, horses, or ropes wound around a horizontal wooden roller formed the support for the shafts, which were frequently tied directly to the treadles. Some looms had *lamms* that enabled the weaver to lower more than one shaft at a time. There were two or four shafts to a loom and the lamms also helped to keep them level. The seat might be a part of the loom frame or a free-standing bench or stool. When not in use, looms were often dismantled and put away or left in an outbuilding until warm weather allowed weaving to resume.[11]

Four-Poster Loom

Also called the barn-frame loom or the bench loom, its framework consisted of four square posts made of solid wood six to seven feet in height. These were joined together in pairs by two long side pieces. See figure 5-1. The seat was generally part of the loom structure.

Single Rear Support Loom

This loom had a short frame and the seat was either separate or attached. See figure 5-2. There was a single, strong supporting unit at the rear on each side. In some cases the heavy side pieces were buttressed by struts at the angles. One cross-piece held up the shafts and another held the overhead beater.

A number of looms from Finnish and Scandinavian communities have side pieces made from naturally curved wood. A tree was carefully chosen for its angle, then slit into two parts which were used for both the sides and the legs of the loom.[12] See figure 5-3. This kind of natural support was thought to make a much stronger frame than the usual joined pieces. See figure 5-4.

Another loom with rear side supports was the Pennsylvania or German loom. Sometimes referred to as the "sleigh" loom, it had deep side "walls" that curved up at each end. The warp beam was higher than the breast beam.[13]

5-4. **Single Support Loom,** courtesy of Vesterheim, the Norwegian-American Museum, Decorah, Iowa.

Central Support Loom with Overhead Beater

In this type of loom, the two side units are located in the middle of the structure. The overhead beater and the shafts are supported by projecting units. See figure 5-4.

Double Support Loom

These looms were often seven feet tall and five feet square. The rear set of support units held the warp beam, and the other set was placed near the center of the structure. The tops of the side units extended forward to carry the beater and the shafts. This design was frequently used in Scandinavian communities. See figure 5-5.

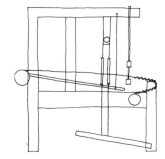

5-5. Double Support Loom.

Low-Slung Beater

In the nineteenth century, loom design was radically altered by reversing the overhead beater and attaching it at the bottom of the loom where it could pivot from pins attached to the sides. This design became the prototype for the treadle loom used by many handweavers today. See figure 5-6. Reversing the beater allowed the housewife to move the loom to the attic where it fit under the eaves. Although the loom became less essential to the functioning of the household, it was always available if needed.[14]

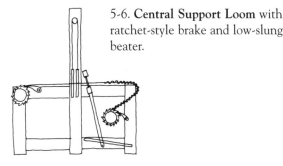

5-6. **Central Support Loom** with ratchet-style brake and low-slung beater.

Innovations

Clever loom adaptations reflect the ingenuity of the craftsman. We know of one man in rural Minnesota who assembled at least a dozen looms for women of his area. Some parts were purchased, others were fashioned in the railroad shop. In certain cases he used ordinary pipes for handles or old steering wheels for cloth-beam crank wheels.

U sually, there was little room for these monstrous pieces of equipment, and so they were often set up in attics and spare rooms. My loom came from such an attic where there was also a huge wheel which could provide power for probably a lathe. The loom was in pieces, long forgotten; a second-hand dealer brought it home and tossed it in a snow bank. It was from here that my father rescued it for me. All of the pieces were there, but we never did find a place for the bed slats that came with it!

Marion L. Channing
The Textile Tools of Colonial Homes

March 15, 1921
The Newcomb Loom Co.
Davenport, Iowa

Dear Sirs:

I want to tell you that I am well pleased with my Weaver's Delight loom. I am kept busy all the time. While I live in a small town, I get trade from the other towns near here. I am having rags sent to me by parcel post from a distance of 75 miles by parties who have seen some of my fancy four-shaft weaves. They pass up their local weavers who have the two-shaft looms and send the work to me.

My buying the Weaver's Delight loom is the best investment I ever made.

Yours truly,
Mr. Eugene Loomis
Hollister, Ohio

Weaving Wisdom: Latest Catalogue of Newcomb Looms
The Newcomb Loom Co.

5-7A. **Weaver's Friend Loom.** The Newcomb Loom Co. version, pipe frame with treadles.

More information on handcrafted looms may be found in books and magazines listed in the *Bibliography*. These sources provide descriptions of old looms, diagrams, and photographs. The diagrams are helpful for putting together an old handcrafted loom or identifying missing parts. You can also see old looms at historical museums and at shows or fairs where demonstrations are given. Regional commemorative events and ethnic festivals may also provide information for research.

Factory-Built Looms

A number of factory-built looms were designed for automatic rag rug and carpet production in the late nineteenth and early twentieth centuries. While the source of inspiration for the design of these automatic production looms is not always evident, several have mechanisms similar to power looms in existence at the time. Certainly these automated machines gave a big boost to home industry and small-scale rug production factories (see Mr. Loomis' letter to the Newcomb Loom Company at left).

Around the time of the Civil War, farm publications indicate that several kinds of self-acting looms were produced in response to the great need for cloth. On these looms, a single motion, such as turning a crank, operated both shafts and shuttles. *Lamb's Family Hand Loom, Mendenhall's Improved, Self Acting Hand Loom,* and *Scofield and Wait's Iron Hand Loom* were among those available.[15] Many looms manufactured for handweavers in the Midwest in the late nineteenth and early twentieth centuries also possess commercial-loom characteristics.

In the 1920s, demand for rag carpeting rose.[16] The carpeting was made by joining rag-woven strips 36" wide. Advertising how they met the carpeting demand quickly and efficiently, manufacturers of automatic looms claimed that a weaver could produce "100 yards a day, 20 yards an hour". According to testimonials witnessed by notary publics, many weavers using fly-shuttle, automatic looms did indeed come close to substantiating this claim.[17] It is certainly true that many more yards of rag carpet could be woven per day on these looms than on the typical counterbalanced hand loom with foot treadles in use early in the century.

Short histories of a few early loom companies are presented in the following paragraphs. This may serve as an introduction to some of the looms, both the automatic and those operated with the feet and hands, which were manufactured specifically for the production of rag rugs.

The quest for information concerning factory-built looms has been difficult and is by no means complete. There is some confusion because looms with the same name have been made by different companies. For example, from 1897 to 1941, the Newcomb Loom Company of Davenport, Iowa, manufactured a *Weaver's Friend* rug loom, a metal, two-shaft loom with wide foot treadles. During part of that period, the Reed Loom Company of Springfield, Ohio lists in its catalogue a *Weaver's Friend* loom that was automatic with a shaft changer. Pointing up the problem, the Reed catalogue warns customers: "Please do not confuse our loom with the gas pipe frame made by another manufacturer who copied our name and calls it 'Weaver's Friend'. Their loom has no automatic harness [shaft] changer, but foot treadles instead."[18] See figure 5-7.

The Oriental Rug Company

Many weavers are familiar with The Oriental Rug Co. of Lima, Ohio. It was established in 1923 by Archie L. Stines in a house next door to his sister, Mrs. Charles Crocket Sr. Archie Stines made looms in his sister's shed and hired men to weave rag rugs on them. He catered to customers who brought their own rags to be woven, as well as to those wanting to buy new rugs. There was such a demand for the rugs that Stines employed his sister's son to help him manufacture looms and weave. They moved from the house to a factory at 214–216 South Central Avenue in 1928, having earlier incorporated as The Oriental Rug Co. with Stines' nephew, Charles H. Crocket Jr., as president until his death in 1988. When Stines passed away in 1962, his duties were assumed by Wanda Lynn, who was employed at The Oriental Rug Co. for 47 years.

In 1970 The Oriental Rug Co. began manufacturing ORCO Looms, basic, weaver-operated machines built primarily for weaving rag rugs. (Some manuals suggest using unspun wool roving or other materials as well.) Oriental sold both *Model 74* (four shafts, six treadles) and *Model 70* (two shafts). Model 74 is copied from the *Cambridge* loom made by the Reed Loom Company, Springfield, Ohio. Model 70 is patterned after *Union Loom No. 36*, made by the Union Loom Works of Boonville, New York. See figure 5-8.

5-7B. **Weaver's Friend Loom.** Reed Loom Co. version with automatic shaft changer instead of treadles. "There is not a loom made which has so many friends as our Weaver's Friend."

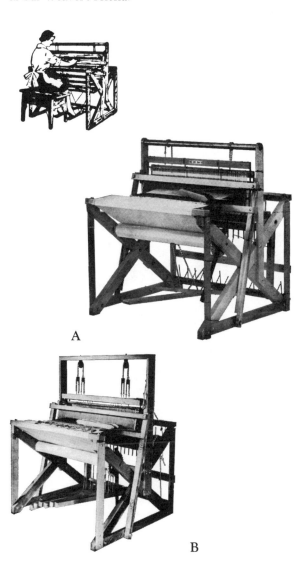

5-8. **Oriental Rug Co. Looms.** A) Model 70, two-shaft loom, designed for rugs. "Your partner in a profitable Home Business." B) Model 74, four-shaft, six-treadle loom, designed for "the fancy weaves such as twill, zig zag, and diamond patterns."

5-9A. Union Custom Loom, distributed by The Carlcraft Co. Their guarantee states that "you will be able to thread the loom, and that you will be easily able to weave first-class work with it—no matter whether you ever saw a loom before or not."

5-9B. The Carlcraft Co. brochure contained very complete information on transporting the loom ("the loom should not be allowed to become wet in being brought from the railroad station"), unpacking it, and even taking it upstairs. "Take the loom, crated as it is as far as the door, and if the loom will not pass through readily, remove the crating, spool rack with treadles, and the long strip above it. . . . In some houses it may be necessary to take the loom apart in order to move it through a narrow hall or up a flight of stairs."

In 1990 The Oriental Rug Co. was merged with the Edgemont Yarn Service and its business operations were moved to Washington, Kentucky.

The Union Loom Works

The Union Loom Works was founded by the Elsaser family. John Elsaser and his son Ben, who died in 1984 at the age of 89, were the original loom builders. Ben's siblings Carl and Edna worked together in **The Carlcraft Company,** supplying rug warp to weavers. In 1984 Carlcraft's warp inventory and customer price list were sold to The Oriental Rug Co.

Edna Elsaser tells this story about the beginnings of Union Loom and Carlcraft:

You've been going to auctions and rummaging through old barns looking for a well-built but slightly dusty loom you can restore for your own use. And at last you've found it! The label says that it was made by the Union Loom Works. Never heard of them, you say? Well then, sit back and let me tell you about John and Ben Elsaser.

John's father had been a handweaver at a time when weaving was a financially practical craft. He loved weaving. Now in 1897 John was making and selling small furniture such as Roman stools. Union Loom Works came into being when John and his son Ben incorporated in 1918. Although John didn't weave much, in the back of his mind he cared about the looms weaving was done on.

The company started with three basic two-shaft counterbalance looms. The advertising leader was called the *Union Home Loom* and sold for $9.90 (or $12.85 if you wanted it prewarped). It was not practical except for hobbyists. The *Union Special Loom* was the most practical and the most popular. It had a weaving width of 36" and sold for $29.50. The third loom was the *Union Custom* with a weaving width of 45". From the very beginning, all Union Looms were designed with rug making in mind.

Another son, Carl, joined the firm in 1923 and did odd jobs around the factory. The Elsasers prospered until the Depression caught up with them; they liquidated the corporation in 1930. Ben continued the manufacture of the looms as a private business until 1969. Union Looms helped many a housewife make ends meet throughout the years, weaving rag rugs as a spare-time business.

John died in 1934, and both sons started new businesses. Carl began The Carlcraft Company, selling carpet warp until 1984. Ben continued making and marketing looms and furniture until 1969. Business for Ben began to pick up, and at peak production, about 1948, he sold 1,800 looms in one year. In the total history of Union Looms, over 40,000 were sold. But the cost of materials for building looms increased and the demand for these simple looms dropped. Sales began to decline and in 1969 Ben discontinued the manufacture of looms. At that time the loom was selling at $110.

Today there's a vacant lot where the bustling Union Loom Works once proudly stood.[20]

The Reed Loom Company

The Reed Loom Company was started in the late 1800s in Springfield, Ohio, by F. C. Reed. See figure 5-10. Its masterpiece was *The Weaver's Friend*, a 45" wide, two-shaft loom with an automatic shaft changer. See figure 5-7B. The change was activated by two beats of the beater. This model was also available in 9, 10, or 12 foot sizes. For those wanting a less expensive loom, the company offered the *Ideal*, weaving up to 36" wide without the automatic change device, or the *Little Dandy*, weaving up to 30" wide. Both were two-shaft looms. Another model was the *Cambridge* loom with four shafts and six treadles. It wove up to 45" wide and was recommended for teaching weaving in schools and colleges.

5-9C. **The Union Special Loom,** a best seller, was advertised in the 1920s for $49.50 complete with 10 yards of warp, ready to weave.

REED LOOM COMPANY
Springfield, Ohio

5-10. **Reed Loom Company Looms.** A) *Ideal* two-shaft rug loom priced at $55 in 1930. B) *Cambridge* four-shaft foot treadle loom. "Being a four-[shaft] loom, the range of work which can be woven on it is almost inexhaustible."

A

B

After Reed's death, Paul Linker continued to build the looms until his death in the 1970s. The looms are no longer being manufactured.[21]

The Newcomb Loom Company

The Newcomb Loom Works was established in Omaha, Nebraska, by Mr. C. N. Newcomb in 1887.[22] Three years later he moved the company to Davenport, Iowa.[23] In the early 1900s William B. Stark took over the business. In 1907 Frank Knierem went to work for Newcomb and by 1919 had purchased the firm. Thus began a long and successful business venture for the Knierem family. Frank served as president until his death in 1954 when his son, Lyman Sr., took over. When Lyman Sr. died in 1961, his son Frank became president.[24] In the early 1980s the Knierem family ceased factory production and some of the loom parts and dies passed to a succession of owners. See figure 5-11A–C.

A catalogue and price list offered in 1893 by C. N. Newcomb cited the increase of weaving speed as his motivation for producing a new rag rug loom. The *Newcomb Fly Shuttle Loom*, states the catalogue, is "The only flying-shuttle rag-carpet loom in existence that is built expressly for rag carpet weaving; the only rag carpet loom with its peculiarly constructed shuttle, that will weave automatically."

The Newcomb shuttle allowed the rag strips to be drawn out in an even manner from pre-packed metal cylinders. A dozen cylinders could be packed at one time; each contained enough weft for 14" of carpeting. To pack the cylinders, the rag strip passed through a guide, over and between two friction rollers, and down into a funnel inserted into the open end of the cylinder. A crank was then turned to fold the rags upon themselves in the funnel. They were then pushed down into the cylinder with a plunger.

Newcomb had studied weaving machinery at the 1893 World's Columbian Exposition. He had also observed many different kinds of looms and corresponded with weavers. His objective was to make a shuttle from which an even, continuous strip of fabric could be drawn just as yarn was drawn from the shuttle on a power loom.[25]

Two other early looms made by the Newcomb Loom Co. were the *Weaver's Friend* and the *Little Daisy*, both with pipe frames. The Weaver's Friend was a counterbalanced loom with two shafts and two wide treadles. It

5-11A. **Newcomb Improved No. 3 Loom,** two-shaft model with fly shuttle. C. N. Newcomb, a local handyman, developed the automatic features of this loom after repairing a handmade loom for a customer.

5-11B. **Shuttle-filler.** With this clever device, rags could be packed tightly into metal cylinders which fit the specially designed rag shuttles of Newcomb's fly shuttle looms.

did not have a fly shuttle. This model was made from 1897 to 1941 when it was discontinued.[26] The Little Daisy had a fly shuttle and the shafts changed with the action of the beater. The first Little Daisy on record was sold in September, 1897, the last in 1943.[27]

The *Newcomb Improved No. 3*, was first manufactured in 1887 and featured in the 1893 catalog.[28] In 1899 it was largely supplanted by the *Weaver's Delight Four Harness, Fly Shuttle Loom.*[29] The Weaver's Delight was similar to the No. 3 in operation but had more shafts for weaving twill and other patterns. About 8,000 Weaver's Delights were made. Each had a number engraved in the wood on the left-side support.

Throughout the years the Knierems made improvements in the structure of the Newcomb looms. They also maintained an active correspondence with their customers, recording when each loom changed owners. The Newcomb Loom Co. sold weaving supplies, kept a full inventory of parts, and circulated a newsletter with weaving hints and contest announcements.

Newcomb looms were sold across the United States and overseas.[30] (Originally Newcomb allowed only one loom in a town or community of less than 1,000 inhabitants. He had a "Five Days' Trial" price and other cash arrangements. The Knierems sold the looms for cash, or on a payment plan.[31]) The looms came fully warped so the customer could weave immediately. Special cams (a set of 14) could be purchased to weave double-width rugs as well as many types of patterns. Early catalogues indicate that equipment was available for cutting old ingrain carpeting into strips for weaving into *fluff rugs*.

During the 1930s the *Studio Art Loom* was developed in response to the demand for a loom for weaving items other than rugs.[32] The Studio Art was a wooden four-shaft, six-treadle loom with rising-shed action meant for handloom weavers who did not have to consider speed and volume production. It was described as especially adapted for pattern weaving, well suited to making "coverlets, draperies, rugs, curtains, and novelties. . . ." Designed by Lyman Knierem, Sr., it was advertised for teaching weaving in schools and colleges, and for occupational therapy work.[33]

There is now a Registry for owners of Newcomb Looms. If you have one, send your name, address, and loom number to: *Historic Looms of America*, Theresa Lee Trebon, 1062 Sterling Rd., Sedro Woolley, WA 98284.

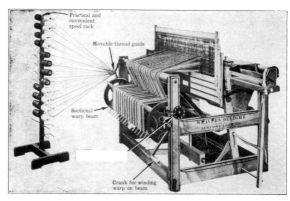

5-11C. **The Weaver's Delight** four-shaft fly-shuttle loom, claimed to be "revolutionizing the home weaving industry". By simply moving the beater back and forth, the warp was released from the warp beam, the shed was changed, and the fabric was advanced on the cloth beam.

Whthat Our Customers Say About Our Looms!
"I am sure glad we took your advice and got the Weaver's Delight Loom. It weaves so fast and tight. We weave 15 yards most days. Can do a 54 inch rug in 15 minutes. We do lots for folks all over the U.S.A. Your step by step instructions are so easy to follow. You folks sure are wonderful to deal with.

Best Regards"
Mrs. Harold Harshbarger
Ohio

Catalogue L, Fly Shuttle and Treadle Hand Looms
The Newcomb Loom Company

5-11D. **Newcomb Studio Art Loom,** a non-automatic loom designed for customers who wanted to do "fancy" weaves. Six treadles allowed greater pattern variation.

Live up to the best that is within you.

Weaver's Manual, Weaver's Delight, 1948
The Newcomb Loom Company

5-12A. Deen Fly Shuttle Loom, *New Reliance* Model, one of the original Deen looms "unequaled for strength and utility".

HEADQUARTERS FOR

CARPET WARP & RUG FILLER

We carry a full line of Carpet Warp and Rug Filler in all colors, at lowest prices. We can ship any amount, any place, quickly. Points east can be supplied from our mill at a saving.
We also have a full stock of dip and stencil dyes and stencils and a full line of weavers supplies. Send for order blanks & latest prices.
Everything for the Weaving Shop!
The Deen Loom Co., Harlan, Iowa.

It is still possible to purchase reprints of Newcomb instruction books. Traditional patterns are given in detail, as well as complete instructions for setting up the loom, warping, loading shuttles, and weaving. Instruction books for the Weaver's Delight Four Harness, Fly Shuttle Loom, the Studio Art Loom, the Little Daisy, the Weaver's Friend, (two-shaft treadle loom), and the Newcomb Loom No. 3 are available. See the *Suppliers List* for ordering information.

The Deen Loom Company

The story of the Deen Loom Company, Harlan, Iowa, is an interesting one of American enterprise. James M. Deen spent his lifetime developing semiautomatic fly shuttle looms for weavers who wanted to set up a home business for selling rag and fluff rugs. Forced to leave school because of ill health, Deen began his weaving career by constructing a copy of an old wooden loom. Not satisfied, he sought for six years to improve the loom's operation. In 1895, when he finally got a model ready for manufacture, he had only $4.25 to his name. He invested $4 in advertising and bought materials for his first dozen looms on credit. As the years went by, more and more looms were sold and Deen continued to make improvements on the loom's mechanism.[34] See figure 5-12A–F.

James Russell Deen, son of the founder of the Deen Loom Company, has provided valuable information on the company history. James Russell Deen was involved in all of the plant operations. A letter from him summarizes the company's operation.

By the time I was born it [the Deen Loom Company] was a well established business with a two-story building covering almost a quarter of a town block. It included all the metal and woodworking machinery required and a cast iron foundry. The second floor was mainly devoted to weaving for the local community. . . .

My father was essentially an inventor. There were numerous models of the looms with differing structures and mechanisms for shifting the [shafts]. The original ones were two-[shaft] using hand-held shuttles. The addition of the fly shuttle mechanism greatly improved the operation of the loom, the shuttle being thrown between the warp web on the back stroke of the beater. The four-[shaft] loom was built in a series of models with different methods of selecting the [shaft] to be lifted involving cams that could be positioned to control the pattern. The late models used the Jacquard principle, a continuous paper strip with punched holes to select the frames that were held up with each stroke of the beater.

The original loom frames were of iron pipe or of wood, then a steel frame loom, the ends being in one piece, formed in a large hydraulic press. The loom in use in the Shelby County Museum [Harlan, Iowa] is one of these, without the fly shuttle. The design of the frames was changed to use flat steel plates with angle iron legs. All of these were well-built and good for years of operation.

The early models used large diameter shallow spools on which the warp was wound, with 15 or more of these across the back of the loom. The warp went around a tension roller and then to the heddles. Later, a single long beam structure was used, with separation pins between which the warp was wound. The take-up roller for the finished rugs had a brake band to control the tension, but later an internal coil spring provided continuous tension as the rug was woven.

In addition to the weaving of rag carpets, Axminster and Brussels type carpets were cut into narrow strips and woven. The strips were twisted so that the nap of the carpet was wrapped around all sides of the strip. These were handwoven in widths up to twelve feet. The strips were put through the shed without the aid of a shuttle. The machine developed for cutting the carpets into narrow strips was very simple. These woven rugs were called fluff rugs; they wore forever but collected a lot of dirt.

The Deen Loom Company was not known outside its field, and today is forgotten in Harlan except for the looms in the Museum. Its business was not closely related to the community, being mail order, except for the work force which was hired. It did not survive World War II, and was in fact hurt severely by the import of the Japanese rag rug before the war.[35]

James M. Deen spent ten years designing and constructing the special machine that cuts and frays the materials for fluff rugmaking. Among his unusual machines for loom building was a mammoth press that cut the steel plates for the sides of the looms. It cut so smoothly that little after-finish was necessary.[36]

5-12B. **Advance Automatic Fly Shuttle Loom.** This two-shaft Deen loom was advertised in a 1928 catalog for $75 cash, or $85 on a time payment plan. It came with a sectional warp beam and a spool rack that fits onto the back beam during warping.

5-12C. **"Advance Loom Goes thru Common Doorways"** was the headline announcing the new, unique folding design of this loom. The brochure stated, "The *Advance* is the only loom made that goes thru doorways in the shape as shown here. . . . This enables it to be taken thru narrow places like stairways and halls without taking apart."

5-12D. In addition to looms and shuttle filling devices, Deen developed equipment for cutting and fraying old ingrain carpeting for re-weaving into *fluff rugs.* Shown is the *Deen Combined Carpet Cutting and Fraying Machine.*

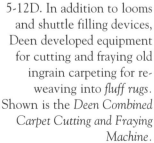

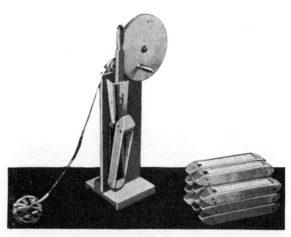

5-12E. Deen Shuttle Filling Machine compressed rags into the shuttle by cranking them through a funnel device. "Filling the shuttles properly is an important matter. The filling will come out just as it goes in, and haphazard work means poor success."

5-12F. Deen Peerless Automatic Fly Shuttle Loom. One of several models with wide weaving width for producing room-sized rugs. "A built-up rug made of carpet rags, with seams, looks like rag carpet. People don't want that kind. They want the seamless rug." A twenty-day home trial plan was offered to prospective buyers.

*D*een *Loom Co.: The Loom arrived Saturday, had to take it apart to get it in my basement but that was easy, and would like to make a kick but cannot find anything to kick about as the loom works just as you said it would, in other words it is a 'He Bear Cat', and will say I am very pleased with it and have a _____ Loom (treadle) for sale or will give it away.*

G. E. Woodruff
Towanda, Pennsylvania

Deen looms equipped with fly shuttles came with a shuttle-filling device. Rags were pushed into a rectangular can with tin plate walls roughened on the inside to prevent the rags from loosening too quickly. This can pivoted out from the shuttle for filling. The loom also had an automatic temple, a small iron roller with threads cut into it like bolt threads. The temple maintained the full width of the rug as it was being woven and was a unique feature of the Deen Loom.[37]

The manufacture and sale of looms increased steadily through the years. New models with complex mechanisms were introduced regularly, ranging in size from 42 inches to 12 feet wide. The *Twill Weave Four Harness Loom* had six shafts, allowing weavers with the proper cam setting to combine two- and four-shaft weaves. From twelve to twenty men were employed in the factory.

Looms could be purchased on a time payment plan with a small down payment. All of the machines and equipment were sold through catalogues that were printed at the factory. Throughout the country, many rug factories apparently began operation with a single Deen Loom.[38]

Two Deen Looms may be seen at the Shelby County Museum, Harlan, Iowa. One is currently in use to weave rugs sold in the Museum. There is one Deen Loom at the Olmsted County Museum in Rochester, Minnesota, and one at the Museum of American Textile History in Lowell, Massachusetts. Three Deen instruction books are available. See *Suppliers List* for ordering information.

The Eureka Loom Company

Dr. William H. Kynett was the inventor and manufacturer of the *Eureka Fly Shuttle Loom*. In the 1870s, during a money crisis, he began to redesign the structure of a hand weaving loom. His wife had purchased it and it was filling the spare room. Dr. Kynett's goal was to produce a loom that would operate more efficiently and take up less space. After experimenting with various designs, he obtained a patent on his plans and began to manufacture the *Eureka Hand Shuttle Loom*, and later, the *Eureka Fly Shuttle Loom*.

Having started to manufacture looms to finance his medical practice, Dr. Kynett in turn sought to provide employment for home-bound women. "His invention was a great blessing to the poor. A large class of women who could not leave home to work installed one of these looms in their humble home, and were able to earn money of which they were so greatly in need."[39]

The Eureka Loom was specifically adapted for the weaving of all kinds of rag carpets. See figure 5-13A–B. One model could weave rugs nine feet square. The firm also dealt wholesale and retail in weaver's reeds, shafts, spools, shuttles, quill wheels, and spinning wheels. In 1895 Eureka offered two carpet looms and five sizes of rug looms, as well as the "quill wheel and shuttle filler" using cans filled with rags. Sales were widespread, in North America, Canada, South America, even South Africa.[40]

In 1893 Dr. Kynett began publishing *The Weaver's Enterprise*, a newsletter "Devoted to the Interests of Handweavers and the Family Circle".[41] The company flourished until 1907, when Dr. Kynett's health declined. He sold the business to the Reed Loom Company of Springfield, Ohio, and moved to Bartow, Florida, where he purchased an orange grove. He died in 1909.[42]

January & Wood Company

No discussion of rag rug weaving, supplies, and equipment would be complete without the *January & Wood Company, Inc.* of Maysville, Kentucky. The Maysville Cotton Mill was founded along the Ohio River in 1824 and was purchased by Mr. January and Mr. Wood in 1851. January bought out Wood in the 1890s, and the company has been operated by descendants of his family since that time.

The January & Wood Co., makers of Maysville Warp since 1879 and Maysville Filler since 1930,

5-13A. **The Eureka Hand Shuttle Loom.** First on the market in 1880, by 1895 Dr. Kynett was allowing trade-ins of this model for his newest fly shuttle loom model.

5-13B. **The Eureka Fly-Shuttle Loom** was a cleverly designed folding model on wheels for moving ease. "The loom is constructed almost wholly of iron, and yet weighs less than the old fashioned wooden loom." But its best feature, according to the catalog, was a cloth beam set back far enough so the weaver's legs wouldn't bump it while weaving.

5-13C. Masthead of the newsletter-catalog published by the Eureka Loom Company.

The Weaver's Enterprise

The Product of the Loom is one of man's first necessities

Devoted to the Interests of Hand Weavers and the Family Circle.

VOL. 3.   BATTLE CREEK, MICH., APRIL, 1895.   NO. 4.

5-14A. **The January & Wood Co.** produced carpet warp and miscellaneous weaving supplies. They published *The Shuttle* newsletter for more than twenty years for members of the Maysville Guild of Home Weavers. It contained patterns, helpful advice, letters, and testimonials from rag rug weavers around the country. Later issues were written and edited by Alice K. and Raymond Cripps, pictured on the cover of the 1964 issue.

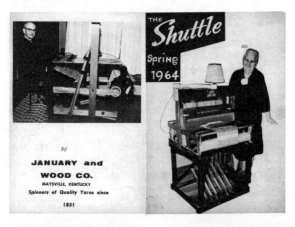

5-14B. Booklets containing projects and instructions published by January & Wood Co.

began publishing *The Shuttle* in 1926. See figure 5-14A–B. For a small subscription fee, this newsletter was sent to rug weavers who used Maysville Warp. The newsletter included projects, pictures, and letters from readers detailing their experiences in selling and weaving. *The Shuttle* reflected the tenor of the times from the 1920s through the Depression and into the years of World War II when January & Wood was committed to the war effort as a producer of cotton twine, twisted cord, and tent rope. In the magazine's last years, Alice K. Cripps was the genial editor, with the help of her husband Raymond. They oversaw the last issue of *The Shuttle* that went out in Spring 1965.

Many thousands of rug weavers received encouragement and helpful advice from this small periodical. Another January & Wood booklet offered to subscribers was the *Weaver's Manual*. An instruction book for beginning weavers, it illustrated many patterns and discussed practical matters of production and distribution.[43] Around 1950, Alice Cripps wrote a pamphlet called *Adventures in Weaving on a 2 harness loom* which sold for 25 cents. The pamphlet contains sales hints and seven lessons featuring patterns and directions for rugs, runners, bags, and placemats. *Adventures in Weaving on a 2 Harness Loom* is still available from the Edgemont Yarn Service. See *Suppliers List* for address.

Edgemont Yarn Service

The Edgemont Yarn Service was started as a retail and mail-order outlet by Jean E. Adair, wife of William Adair, head of January & Wood. Jean designed crochet, knitting, and weaving patterns for the company and was in charge of publishing *The Shuttle* magazine from 1957 to 1965. Managed by William and Jean Adair's daughter, Belinda Bothman, Edgemont Yarn Service offers items manufactured by January & Wood, as well as new warp sizes and weft materials. In 1986 Edgemont purchased *Tinkler & Co.* from E. F. Shaw and added that company's warp to their line. (Tinkler & Co. had been operated by the Tinkler family in the Philadelphia area from the 1940s to the 1970s.) In 1990 the business operations of *The Oriental Rug Co.* were merged with Edgemont Yarn Service, who continues making ORCO's Model 70 and 74 looms in Washington, Kentucky.

Other Loom Companies

There is evidence that looms manufactured by *J. L. Hammett & Co.* of Cambridge, Massachusetts, established in 1863, were used for rag rugs. Their advertisement in *The Handicrafter* (April/May 1929) shows a sturdy four-shaft treadle loom suitable for such work. See figure 5-15. Contemporary newsletters also mention *W. B. Kirkpatrick,* Arrowsmith, Illinois, who built the *Kirk Loom* at the turn of the century, and *The Baker Loom Company,* Council Bluffs, Iowa, manufacturer of "the best loom on earth".[44]

Undoubtedly, many more loom companies were actively involved in making looms suitable for rag weaving. Further research should reveal the whereabouts of these looms and their inventors.

Loom Manuals

A book of instructions and projects was included with each factory-built loom. These manuals were very complete, with detailed directions on how to get the loom into the house, how to set it up, and how to weave on it. There were diagrams for preparing rags and color and design recommendations. Various patterns were presented with suggestions for warps and wefts. Instructions were included for selling and pricing the rugs. These booklets provide today's weaver with a wealth of information, as well as an interesting view of the early years of the twentieth century. In an effort to preserve the manuals' classic patterns, several have been included in the projects in *Chapter Four.*

Many manuals are available from the Loom Manual Library. See *Suppliers List* for ordering information.

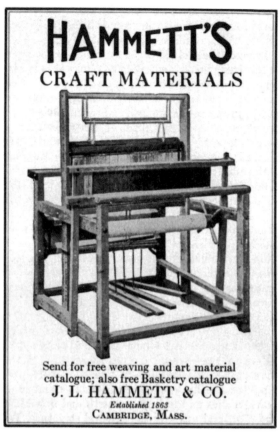

5-15. Advertisement for the *Hammett Loom,* 1929.

WEAVING
as a
Spare Time
Occupation

SPARE TIME PAYS BIG PROFITS

As you are paid so much a yard or so much a rug for weaving, the amount of money you earn will of course depend upon how much and how fast you weave. Weavers quite generally now charge 50 cents a yard for ordinary weaving such as rag carpet. In some localities the price is more. This does not include the warp; you charge extra for the warp, depending upon what it costs you. Prices on warp fluctuate, but at present prices it is around 18 cents a yard, making the charge for weaving and warp 68 cents a yard.

Illustrations from Union Loom Catalog, ca. 1930, extolling the advantages of a home weaving business using Union looms. "Work usually demands your full time every day or it does not pay very well. But weaving solves this problem. It will surprise you to see how quickly and conveniently you can earn money with a loom in your home."

Is Weaving Profitable?

We can truthfully say that it is. We do say that all who purchase looms do not make a success of it. This is the sole fault of the user and not the fault of the loom. The weaving business is like any other business. It is up to the person to get the profits out of it, as the looms have no brains to manage the business for you. We know of no other business that brings in so much on the investment as the making of rugs with our looms.

The beauty about this business is that it is not necessary for you to devote your entire time to it. Of course, the profits depend upon the amount of time that is devoted to it. It will add considerable to any one's income even if they devote only part of their time to it. Another thing in this business is that most of your work comes to you without even soliciting it. You can always grow in the business. Many start with one loom, making rag rugs, rag carpets, etc., then they add on other looms until they have a fully equipped weaving factory.

Many blind people, as well as other afflicted ones, find a profitable business with our looms. Many widows have gratefully thanked us for starting them in the business, which enabled them to make a good, honest living.

Article in Reed Loom Company brochure, ca. 1945.

Notes

1. Kagao Muraoka and Kitchieman Okamura. *Folk Arts and Crafts of Japan*. Tokyo: Heibonsha; New York: Weatherhill, 1973. Figures 128, 129.
2. John Hinchcliff and Angela Jeffs. *Rugs from Rags*. London: Orbis Publishing, 1977, page 13.
3. Geraldine Niva Johnson. *Weaving Rag Rugs: A Women's Craft in Western Maryland*. Knoxville: University of Tennessee Press, 1985. Harold B. Burnham and Dorothy K. Burnham. *Keep Me Warm One Night: Early Handweaving in Eastern Canada*. Toronto: University of Toronto Press, 1972. See both sources for information on early rag rug traditions in America and in Canada.
4. Rita Adrosko. "American Coverlet Looms", in: Shaeffer, Margaret. *Made in New York State: Handwoven Coverlets 1820–1860*, page 2.
5. Osma Gallinger Tod and Josephine Couch Del Deo. *Designing and Making Handwoven Rugs*. New York: Dover Publications, 1957, page 131.
6. Burnham and Burnham, page 84.
7. Tod and Del Deo, page 130.
8. Beverly Gordon. *Shaker Textile Arts*. Hanover, Massachusetts: University Press of New England, 1980, pages 90–103.
9. *Weaving Wisdom*. Davenport, Iowa: The Newcomb Loom Co., date unknown, page 8.
10. *The Shuttle*. Maysville, Kentucky: January & Wood Co. Copies from 1942 to 1944. Published for members of the Maysville Guild of Home Weavers.
11. Nancy Dick Bogdonoff. *Handwoven Textiles of Early New England*. Harrisburg, PA: Stackpole Books, 1975, pages 56–60. Eric C. Broudy. *The Book of Looms*. New York: Van Nostrand Reinhold, 1979, pages 160–161. Correspondence with Gene E. Valk, Handweaver, Gloversville, NY. March 7, 1986. Marion Channing. *The Textile Tools of Colonial Homes*. Marion, Massachusetts: Reynolds-DeWalt, 1969, pages 43–46.
12. Gertrude Grenander Nyberg. *Lanthemmens Vävstolar: Studier Redskap for Husbehövsvavning*. Stockholm: Nordiska Museet, 1975, page 328.
13. Mary C. Saylor. "A Reflection of the Past", *Shuttle, Spindle & Dyepot*, Volume VII, No. 3. Summer 1976, pages 26–27.
14. Broudy, pages 160–161: Correspondence, Gene E. Valk, May 12, 1986.
15. Victor L. Hilts and Patricia A. Hilts. "Not for Pioneers Only: The Story of Wisconsin's Spinning Wheels", in *Wisconsin Magazine of History*. August, 1982, pages 13–15. See footnotes for farm journals.
16. *Weaving Wisdom*. Davenport, Iowa: The Newcomb Loom Co., ca. 1921, page 8.
17. C. N. Newcomb. *Catalogue and Price List of the Newcomb Flying Shuttle Rag Carpet Loom*. Davenport, Iowa: Ed Borcherdt, Printer, September 1893, cover and testimonials.
18. *Looms*. Springfield, Ohio: Reed Loom Company, page 4.
19. Correspondence, Wanda Lynn, Manager, The Oriental Rug Co., February 14, 1985.
20. Correspondence, Carl and Edna Elsaser, October 29, 1985. Also, "Union Loom Works", *Handwoven*, Volume II, No. 3. May 1981, page 28.
21. Correspondence, Wanda Lynn, February 14, 1985.
22. "Saengerfest Souvenir", *Davenport Illustrated*. Davenport, Iowa: The Democrat Co. Printers, July 1898.

23. "These looms are still put together by hand", *The Sunday Dispatch*. Moline, Illinois. January 23, 1977.
24. "Competition? What's That?" *Sunday Times Democrat*. Davenport, Iowa. July 4, 1965.
25. C. N. Newcomb. *Catalogue and Price List of the Newcomb Flying Shuttle Rag Carpet Loom*. Davenport, Iowa: Ed. Borcherdt, Printer, September, 1893, pages 1, 3, 6, 7.
26. Record Books for the *Weaver's Friend Loom*. The Newcomb Loom Co. (Courtesy of Theresa Lee Trebon.)
27. Record Books for the *Little Daisy Loom*. The Newcomb Loom Co. (Courtesy of Theresa Lee Trebon.)
28. Record Books for the *Improved No. 3 Loom*. The Newcomb Loom Co. (Courtesy of Theresa Lee Trebon.)
29. Record Books for the *Weaver's Delight Loom*. The Newcomb Loom Co. (Courtesy of Garland Tickle.)
30. *Sunday Times Democrat*, July 4, 1965.
31. C. N. Newcomb, page 12. (1893 catalogue.) Copy of an agreement drawn up in 1949 with The Newcomb Loom Co. for purchase of *Weaver's Delight Fly Shuttle Carpet Loom* for monthly payments. See old catalogues for payment plans and special offers.
32. Record Books of the *Studio Art Loom*. The Newcomb Loom Co. (Courtesy of Theresa Lee Trebon.)
33. The Newcomb Loom Co., *Looms, Catalogue O*. Davenport, Iowa, date unknown, page 9. An interview with Georgia Knierem and her son, Frank Knierem, on May 15, 1986, provided much of the material in this history. The Knierems generously shared clippings, catalogues, photographs, instruction books, and letters from the early days of the Newcomb Loom Co.
34. P. B. Brown. "A Rag-Carpet Business Romance", *The Iowa Magazine Section*, Vol. 7, August 16, 1923, page 611. (Clipping provided by Harlan Community Library, Harlan, Iowa.)
35. Correspondence with James Russell Deen, May 6, 1986.
36. Brown, Vol. 7, page 611.
37. James M. Deen. *Weaving for Profit*. Harlan, Iowa: Deen Loom Company, date unknown, pages 8, 9, 12. Catalogue with color illustrations.
38. E. S. White. *History of Shelby County, Iowa*. Indianapolis, Indiana: B. F. Bowen & Co., Inc. 1915, page 1093.
39. "The Hand Loom Factory", in *The Daily Journal*, Battle Creek, Michigan, 10 June 1910, page unknown, clipping file, Willard Library, Battle Creek, Michigan. Other clippings include: "Dr. W. H. Kynett", *The Daily Journal*, 16 August 1894, page unknown. All the information in this paragraph is from a group of clippings provided by the Willard Library.
40. "The Eureka Loom Co.", clipping, 18 January, 1894, clipping file, Willard Library, Battle Creek, Michigan.
41. "Moonbeams", *Moon*. Battle Creek, Michigan, 6 September 1893, clipping file, Willard Library, Battle Creek, Michigan.
42. "The Hand Loom Factory", and "The Eureka Loom Co." These articles tell of Eureka's success in manufacturing looms, sashes, doors, blinds, scrolls, and turned work. Dr. Kynett then lists the equipment in the shop, and announces that it is all for sale or trade for good real estate in or out of the city.
43. See the *Weaver's Manual*, published for members of the Maysville Guild of Home Weavers by January & Wood Co., Maysville, Kentucky.
44. *The Weaver's Herald*, Volume XI, Number 2, February 1902, page 2. Advertising Circular, The Baker Loom Company.

Y̶ou who are using the old fashioned Barn Loom (as it is called) please note carefully the testimonials and affidavits following:

Niantic, Illinois, June 6, 1891

C. N. Newcomb, Davenport, Iowa: I was glad to hear that I won second prize, and was glad none of the ladies could beat me. . . . The first hour I wove 14 yards, but towards the last I was so tired that I could not keep it up. . . . Almost everyone in town was in while I was weaving. I was watched with much interest by everybody. I will answer all correspondence with pleasure, as before, I remain, Very truly yours, E. Alice Claypool State of Illinois, Macon County

Personally appeared before me, John P. Ferris, a Notary Public in and for said county and state, E. Alice Claypool, well known to me to be entitled to credit, and on her oath deposeth and says that she has woven on C. N. Newcomb's Flying Shuttle Carpet Loom one hundred three and one-half (103½) yards of rag carpet in 10 hours. Subscribed and sworn to before me this 28th day of May, A.D. 1891.

John P. Ferris, Notary Public

The Newcomb Loom Company

Appendix I
Basic Warping Methods

Warping is the process of measuring and installing threads on the loom, keeping them parallel, in order, and under similar tension. The various warping procedures devised by weavers are a series of logical steps to achieve this end. For beginning weavers, warping may seem complicated, but it becomes routine with practice.

The first step in warping is to measure all the warp threads by winding them in a figure eight on a *warping board* or *warping reel*. See figure A-1. The warp is then taken to the loom. The steps in "dressing" the loom involve spreading the warp to the desired width in the *reed*, or in a device called a *raddle*; attaching the warp to the *back beam* and winding it on under tension; bringing individual warp ends through the *heddles* and reed; and, finally, tying the warp onto the *cloth beam*. The exact order of these steps will vary, depending on whether you use the *Back-to-Front Method* or the *Front-to-Back Method* with your loom. *Tying-on* a new warp to the end of an existing warp is an alternate method for continuing with projects of the same size and threading. The handling of extremely long warps is dealt with in *Appendix II*.

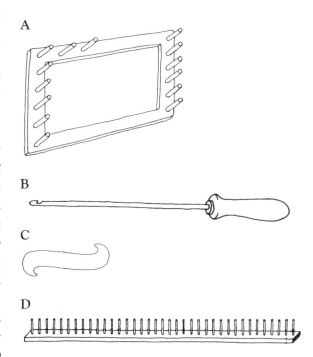

A-1. **Warping equipment.** A) Warping Board. B) Threading Hook. C) Reed or Sley Hook. D) Raddle.

Using a Warping Board

Determining Warp Length

These directions are for the warp described in *Chapter One: Getting Started*. See that chapter for warp length calculation.

At 4½ feet long, a back door/kitchen sink rug requires 3 yards of warp in length, set at 12 e.p.i. The standard width of such a rug is about 28 inches. Calculate the number of warp ends needed as follows:
12 e.p.i. × 28 inches wide = 336 ends
336 ends × 3 yards = 1008 yards of warp.

Because there are 800 yards on an 8-ounce tube of carpet warp, you'll need two tubes of warp in the same color for this rug.

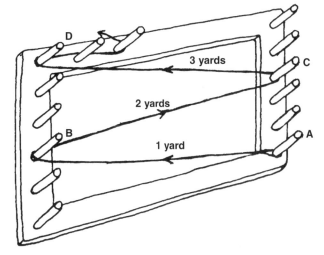

A-2. **Winding the warp.** Tie on yarn at peg **A**. Zigzag warp from pegs **B** to **C** to **D**, measuring 3 yards.

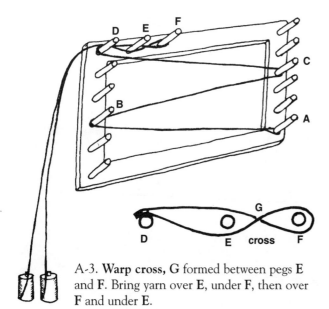

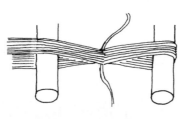

A-3. **Warp cross, G** formed between pegs **E** and **F**. Bring yarn over **E**, under **F**, then over **F** and under **E**.

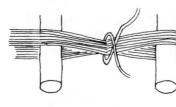

contrasting thread

A-4. **Counting thread** placed over groups of 24 warp ends at the cross.

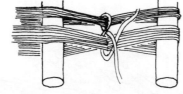

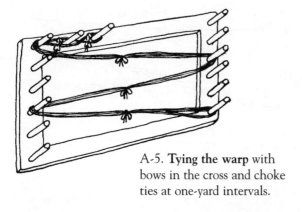

A-5. **Tying the warp** with bows in the cross and choke ties at one-yard intervals.

Winding the Warp

Measure all the warp threads on a *warping board*, a sturdy wooden frame with pegs along each side and across the top or bottom. See figure A-2. The distance from peg to peg across the width of the board is usually one yard. For a three-yard warp, the threads need to travel across the board three times.

1. *Use two spools of carpet warp.* Place each one in a bucket or coffee can to prevent them from rolling around on the floor.

2. *Tie the two warp ends together,* making a loop. Follow figure A-2. Slip the loop over peg **A** at the bottom right and bring the two threads across the board to a peg on the left, then across to a peg on the right. Continue crossing back and forth for the desired length (three yards).

3. *Form a warp cross* (**G**) at the top of the board by winding over and under extra pegs (**E** and **F**). See figure A-3.

4. *Retrace the path of the warp back across the board* to the bottom peg. Keep the threads pushed down toward the base of the pegs, overlapping somewhat to prevent bending and possibly breaking the pegs.

5. End the warp by tying the threads onto peg **A.**

Counting Thread

After winding about 30 ends, add a counting thread in the warp cross area. See figure A-4.

1. Place a short piece of contrasting color scrap yarn behind all the threads at the cross **G** and count them by two's.

2. Cross the ends of the scrap yarn over each group of 24 threads.

3. Continue winding the warp and crossing each bunch of 24 with the scrap yarn. For a rug 28" wide, there will be 14 bunches of 24 threads each. (14 × 24 = 336 ends.) Each bunch of 24 threads will fill 2" in the reed at 12 e.p.i. (2" × 14 = 28" wide).

Tying the Warp

The warp must be tied securely in several places to keep the threads in order before removal from the board.

• *Cross ties:* Take short pieces of strong yarn and tie them securely around the four segments of the warp cross (at pegs **E** and **F**) with a bow knot. See figure A-5.

• *Choke ties*: Make choke ties at one-yard intervals along the warp by wrapping a piece of strong yarn tightly around the warp twice, then tying a bow knot.

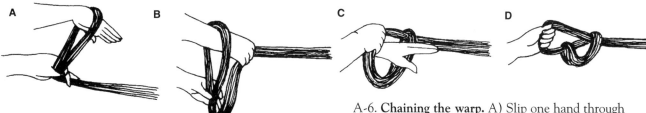

Chaining the Warp

Starting at peg **A,** slide the warp off the bottom peg and slip the loop onto your wrist. *Chain the warp* as illustrated. See figure A-6. The process is similar to crocheting, using your hand as a hook and pulling a new loop through the previous one. Continue chaining the warp up to the cross. *Do not pull the end through the last loop.*

A-6. **Chaining the warp.** A) Slip one hand through the end loops. B) Grasp the warp with the same hand. C) Pull a loop through the loop on your wrist. D) Put your hand through this new loop. E and F) Repeat the grasping and pulling process.

Dressing the Loom: Back-to-Front Method

This is a good method for handling long chain warps. The warp is put directly onto the back beam first, then threaded through heddles and reed. A raddle is used on the back beam to hold the warp threads at the proper width while they are wound onto the beam.

Positioning and Spreading the Warp

1. *Release the hooks* on the heddle bars to slide the heddles to the left.

2. *Place a raddle on the back beam*, tied in place with cord or yarn scraps.

3. *Center the warp.* Mark the center of the raddle and measure 14" (or half your project width) to the right to locate your starting point.

4. *Insert lease sticks into the cross.* Tie them securely and pass them through the shafts from the front of the loom. See figure A-7.

5. *Suspend the lease sticks* behind the shafts from the top of the loom. Keep the counting thread that separates the bunches of 24 ends. Remove the cross ties (but not the choke ties).

6. *Spread the warp* to 28" by separating each bunch of 24 warp ends. Starting on the right side, take the first bunch and slip the end loops over the nail on the raddle at the 14" mark. Place loops over every other nail

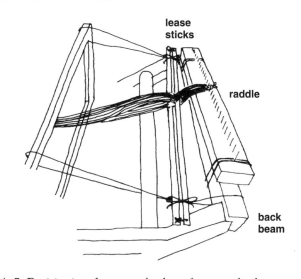

A-7. **Positioning the warp,** back-to-front method. Raddle tied to back beam, warp cross in lease sticks, and tied in place in front of raddle.

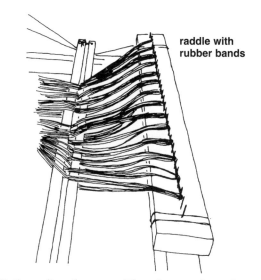

A-8. **Spreading the warp.** Threads spaced evenly in the raddle, rubber bands holding threads in place.

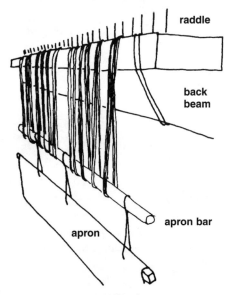

A-9. **Apron rod inserted** in end loops; warp ready to wind onto back beam.

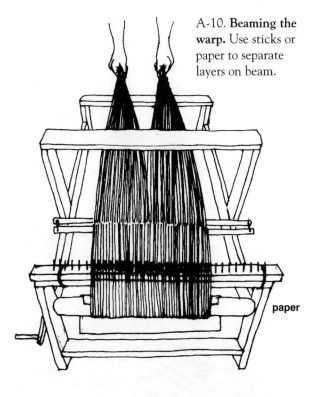

A-10. **Beaming the warp.** Use sticks or paper to separate layers on beam.

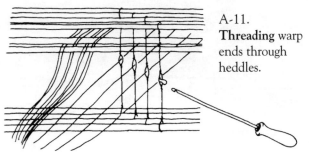

A-11. **Threading** warp ends through heddles.

all the way across the raddle. Loosen or remove counting ties as loops are placed over nails. There should be 12 ends in each space. Stretch rubber bands from nail to nail on top of the warp on the raddle to keep the threads in place. See figure A-8.

7. *Insert the apron rod* through the end loops in the warp, remembering to place apron cords at appropriate intervals. See figure A-9.

8. *Adjust tension.* Go to the front of the loom and untie the first choke tie around the warp. Grasp the warp at the next tie and tug it firmly to straighten the threads on the apron rod.

Beaming the Warp

Advance the warp beam slowly during this stage. If working alone, you will need to alternate between winding at the back of the loom and pulling on the warp at the front beam.

1. Divide the warp chain in two and hold the parts like reins at the front of the loom. Shake the warp, removing ties as they come forward during winding. Tug firmly after each half yard.

2. Wind a half yard at a time, inserting cardboard, paper, or sticks to keep the warp layers separate. See figure A-10. The warp should be fairly tight on the beam.

3. Watch for snags and knots at the cross while winding. Usually a combination of shaking and tugging will be enough to free snarls. Some weavers use a strumming motion with one hand across the warp to help loosen tangles.

4. Stop winding when the end of the warp comes up to the breast beam. Trim the warp ends evenly across.

Threading

The warp cross suspended in the lease sticks will aid in threading the heddles in the proper order.

1. *Remove breast beam and beater,* if possible. Place a stool or chair in front of the shafts. Adjust the warp cross on the lease sticks so that it is at eye level behind the heddles.

2. *Draw each warp end through a heddle* using a threading hook and moving from right to left. See figure A-11. Take the threads in order from the cross intersection. Choose either thread from the pair in the cross. If the loom has only 2 shafts, thread a heddle on shaft 1, then shaft 2, then 1, then 2, etc. On a four-

shaft loom, thread the heddles on shafts 1 through 4 consecutively (1,2,3,4,1,2,3,4).

3. *Check threading order* after each group of 12 ends. Tie the group in a loose slip knot and push it to the right. See figure A-12.

4. When all ends are threaded and tied, replace breast beam and beater.

Sleying the Reed

The reed acts as a warp spacer and as a beater.

1. *Find the center* of the reed by measuring and mark it with a piece of thread.

2. *Find your starting place* by measuring 14" to the right of center (or half your project width).

3. *Insert a reed hook* at the 14" mark between dents in the reed, hook the first heddle thread, and pull it through the reed. See figure A-13.

4. Continue working from right to left, stopping to check for skipped slots or doubled threads.

5. Remove the raddle and lease sticks.

Tying-On

In this final step, the warp ends are tied to the front apron bar.

*Pull up the front apron rod and secure the ratchet on the cloth beam. Tie 1" bunches of threads to the apron rod. See figure A-14.

Keep the tension even by starting to tie on in the center. Tie several bunches to the right, then several to the left, working toward each edge. The end bunches should contain less than 12 warp ends. Check the warp tension by running the palm of your hand over the warp behind the beater. If the warp is loose in any area, tighten the entire warp by starting at the center again.

For further information on this method of warping see *Beginning Loom Weaving*, a manual and companion videotape by Joyce Marquess Carey. Both may be obtained from The Handweavers Guild of America, Two Executive Concourse, Suite 201, 3327 Duluth Highway, Duluth, GA 30136-3373. The manual may be ordered separately.

Dressing the Loom: Front-to-Back-Method

This method works well for handling shorter warps (from two to five yards). The reed is sleyed first, acting as the warp spreader, and the shafts are threaded *before* the warp is wound onto the back beam. Follow the basic instructions for planning your warp, determining

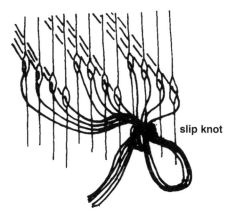

A-12. **Tie groups** of 12 warp ends together temporarily in a loose slip knot.

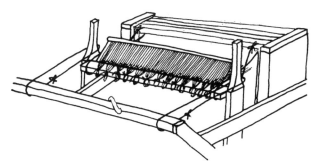

A-13. **Sleying the reed** using a reed hook or sley hook. Groups of ends are tied in slip knots.

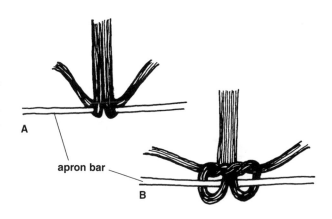

A-14. **Tying-on to a apron bar.** Divide each bunch of warp ends. Bring the two ends over and around the apron bar to tie in a surgeon's knot or double-wrap knot.

the amount needed, and winding the warp on a board or reel. Once the warp is wound, continue in the following manner:

• Make the ties. Tie the cross by putting a string through it or put lease sticks in directly. Then make a choke tie 30 to 36 inches from the cross. Make choke ties at regular intervals to the end of the warp. Tie a contrasting color string through the loops at both ends of the warp for cutting guides.

• Chain the warp.

Spreading the Warp

Sley the reed first as follows:

1. *Tie the lease sticks* containing the warp cross securely onto the breast beam. Position the warp so it will be centered in the reed. See figure A-15.

2. *Cut the end loops* of the warp.

3. *Draw the warp ends through the reed* from front to back, taking them in order from the cross.

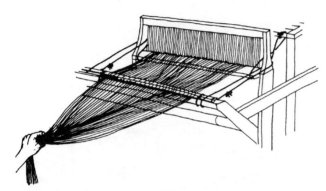

A-15. **Spreading the warp,** front-to-back method. Lease tied to front beam. End loops cut and drawn through the reed.

Threading

Sit at the back of the loom, facing the shafts and thread the ends in order from the reed through the heddles.

• Thread each warp end through a heddle on each shaft in order from front to back, making sure not to cross threads between the reed and the heddles.

• As each pattern repeat is threaded through the heddles, tie it in a loose knot.

Tying-On to the Warp Beam Rod

When threading is completed, pull the ends through to the back of the loom and tie them in bunches to the warp beam rod. See figure A-16. Distribute the bunches evenly to center the warp.

Beaming the Warp

The warp can now be wound through the loom onto the back beam.

1. *Cut the ties* holding the warp to the breast beam and remove lease sticks. At the front of the loom, tug on the warp chain to straighten the warp and get the ends in order. Avoid combing with the fingers. See figure A-10.

2. Begin *winding at the back of the loom.* Cover the knots on the warp beam with cardboard or flat sticks

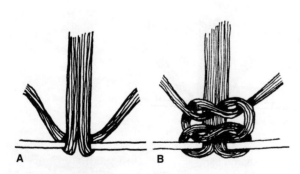

A-16. **Tying-on to a warp beam rod.** Bring two groups of six warp ends over and around the warp beam rod to tie in a square knot.

on the first turn. When the warp begins to resist in front, go to the front of the loom and tug again until the threads straighten out.

3. *Continue winding*, untying the choke ties as necessary. Insert cardboard or sticks as needed to keep the layers of warp separated on the beam. Occasionally grasp the warp chain and pull hard.

Tying-On to the Cloth Beam Rod

When the warp is wound on, leave about 12" in front of the reed. Tie the ends to the cloth beam rod using the method shown in figure A-14. Begin tying at the center and work outward toward the selvedges. Check the tension and retie as needed.

Tying a New Warp onto an Existing Warp

If the same threading and the same number of ends are to be used for the next project, the new warp can be tied onto the old warp. When the finished rug is removed from the loom, cut the ends *in front of the reed*. Tie the cut ends in loose bunches to keep them from slipping out of the reed.

1. *Prepare the new warp as described above.* Tie contrasting-color string through the loops at both ends of the warp for cutting guides. Place lease sticks through the cross.

2. *Tie the lease sticks* securely to the breast beam and cut the warp at the end ties. Spread the warp cross on the lease sticks. See figure A-17.

3. *Tie each new warp end to an old end* starting at one side and working across. Use a weaver's knot, square knot or overhand knot.

4. *Ease the knots through* the reed and the heddles in small groups.

5. *Wind the warp onto the warp beam*, placing flat sticks or cardboard strips on the beam as you wind to keep the layers separate. Tug on the new warp occasionally to keep the tension even. Shake to loosen tangles. Wind until the warp is about 12" beyond the breast beam.

6. *Tie the warp ends onto the front apron bar.* See figure A-14. Begin tying in the center and work toward each edge, checking the tension as you go.

> W hen *putting the warp on the roller, if there happens to be some string or two loose, don't 'milk the loose' or try to pull those warps toward you and into the braid [warp chain]. Instead, allow them to roll loosely on the roller. They will find their place while you keep on weaving.*
>
> Rora Strom
> Two Harbors, Minnesota

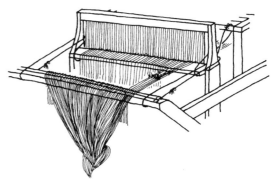

A-17. **Tying a new warp** onto an existing warp. Lease sticks are fastened to the breast beam.

Selected Bibliography:
Chandler, Deborah. *Learning to Weave*, Revised Edition. Loveland, Colorado: Interweave Press Inc., 1995.
Garrett, Cay. *Warping All By Yourself*. Sonoma, California: The Handweaver Press, 1977 (available from Interweave Press).
Scorgie, Jean. "Long Warps", *Handwoven*, Volume 6, No. 2 (March/April 1985), pages 43–45.
Tidball, Harriet. *The Weavers Book*. New York: Collier Books, 1976, chapter "Dressing the Loom".

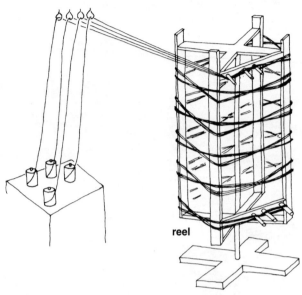

A-18. **Using a warping reel** or mill. Overview of winding process.

Appendix II

Handling Very Long Warps

Using a Large Reel or Mill

This warping technique has been observed in northern Minnesota. It seems to follow the traditional Swedish warping procedures found in Cyrus-Zetterström, *Manual of Swedish Handweaving*. The *warping mill*, or *reel* helps prepare very long warps (60 to 90 yards). It may be used with a small stand or bench with nails to hold the tubes of warp.

Measuring the Warp (See figure A-18.)

1. *Make a guide string.* Calculate the length of warp needed and cut a piece of string the required warp length. Tie this onto the first bottom peg, wind it around the reel, and place the top pegs so that the guide string reaches the last one.

2. *Use four tubes of carpet warp* (either 1/2- or 1-pound tubes). Place them on a spool rack or on large nails set into a bench. If several colors are to be used, place them on the rack in order, i.e., for Log Cabin pattern, use two tubes of color A, two tubes of color B.

3. *Take one end from each spool* and thread it through a screw eye placed in the ceiling or on a board above the tubes.

4. *Tie the four ends together* and slip them around the first bottom peg on the reel. See figure A-19A. Wind them around the reel following the guide string until you reach the desired length, then go around the set of three pegs at the top to form the warp cross. See figure A-19B. (Some weavers make a cross at each end; one cross is used for placing warp threads in the raddle, the other for the threading.)

5. *Adjust tension* after the first trip around the reel. Wind the warp so that you form a figure-eight across each side of the reel. Wind first over the top edge of warp, then over the bottom edge. This will keep the warp ends from sagging. Proceed to wind the four ends together as many times around as are needed to reach the desired number of ends in the warp.

6. *Count out groups of warp ends* corresponding to the number needed per section in your raddle. Wrap these

with a counting thread as described in figure A-4.

7. *Tie the cross* so that lease sticks may be slipped in easily. See figure A-19C.

8. *Remove the bottom peg* and chain the warp off the reel as described in figure A-6. Be sure to maintain tension as the warp unwinds. Store the warp in a basket or box.

Alternate Methods for Measuring a Guide String

1. Measure the warp length needed from one tube of warp and mark this thread by tying on a piece of contrasting-color thread every 10 yards. Wind this thread back onto the tube and place it on the holder with the three other tubes. Begin winding the reel, stopping to form the cross when the last colored marker is reached.

2. Measure the circumference of the reel and wind the four warp ends around it the required number of times. (On a three-yard reel, wind 10 times around for a 30-yard warp.)

Placing Warp on the Loom

For the Back-to-Front Method, you will need an assistant to handle very long warps.

1. Remove the reed from the beater and place a raddle in its place. Attach the rod to the warp beam. Slip one end of the warp onto the rod.

2. Separate the warp into raddle sections. Bring the warp forward over the front beam and back underneath the loom. See figure A-20.

3. One person sitting at the back of the loom holds the warp under tension while the other person winds it onto the warp beam, placing at least three sticks to a turn. It is important to watch carefully for twisted ends at the cross and at the raddle.

4. When you've finished winding, remove the raddle. Cut the threads at this end of the warp.

5. Knot groups of ends loosely. Position lease sticks behind the heddles so the cross can be reached for threading. Sit facing the loom. Remove breast beam, if possible.

6. Draw ends through the heddles with the threading hook, then draw the ends through the reed with a sley hook. Tie groups of threads to the front apron rod which is attached to the cloth beam.

Cyrus-Zetterström, Ulla. *Manual of Swedish Handweaving.* Stockholm: LTs förlag, 1950. Third English Edition, 1984. Available form Glimåkra Looms 'n Yarns. See *Suppliers List*.

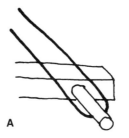

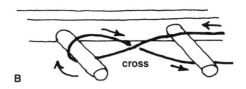

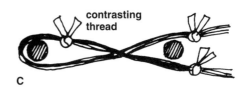

A-19. **The warp cross.** A) Starting. B) Forming the warp cross. C) Tying the cross.

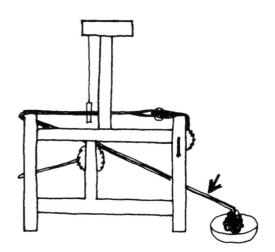

A-20. **Dressing the loom.** Warp chain in position for beaming.

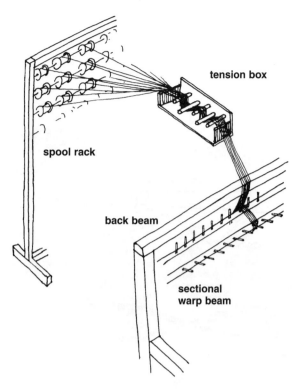

tension box

spool rack

back beam

sectional
warp beam

A-21. **Spool rack** placed behind loom. The warp ends go through the tension box (attached to back beam of loom) and are wound onto a section of the warp beam.

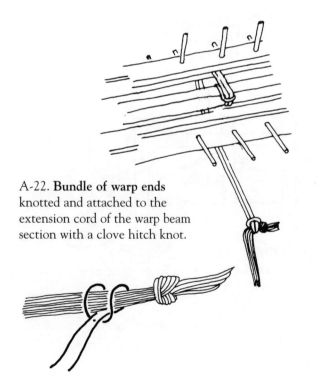

A-22. **Bundle of warp ends** knotted and attached to the extension cord of the warp beam section with a clove hitch knot.

Sectional Warping

If you have a loom with a sectional warp beam, sectional warping is a fast method for putting on long warps. The warp thread is wound directly from tube to loom. *Sections* on a beam are usually 2" wide. Your *spool rack* should hold the number of tubes of warp needed to fill one section at the desired number of ends per inch. If your rug is set at 12 e.p.i., you'll need a 24-tube rack. You must also attach a *tension box* or guide to the back beam to help you wind the warp ends into each section with an even tension. See figure A-21.

Beaming Procedure

1. Place the spool rack holding 24 tubes of warp behind the loom. See figure A-21.

2. *Center the warp.* Count the number of warp sections in the rug. For a 28" rug, use the center 14 sections. Tie a cord to the warp beam in each section.

3. Thread a warp end from each tube through the tension box spacer, over and under the tension box pegs and space them evenly in the tension box reed. The width of the spread in the reed should be slightly less than 2" to allow for the width of the pegs on the beam. If necessary, put more than one end per dent.

4. Knot the bundle of warp ends as close to the end as possible.

5. Begin at either of the outside sections. Tie the cord in a clove hitch around the knotted warps. See figure A-22. Position the tension box on the beam directly above the section to be filled.

6. Turn the beam, watching carefully to see that the section fills evenly. Check to make sure you are turning the beam in the right direction. If the warp piles up unevenly, adjust the position of the tension box. Count each revolution of the beam as you fill the first section. All the other sections should be filled with the *same number of turns* to avoid tension problems in the warp.

7. When the section is full, place a piece of masking tape across the warp ends to keep them in order. The tape takes the place of a cross. Cut the warp one inch beyond the tape. Pin the tape into the filled section. See figure A-23.

8. Move the tension box to the other outside section and fill it. Work your way to the center, filling a section on either side.

9. When all the sections are full, remove the pins from each section and pull the warp up over the back beam toward the shafts. Lay a long stick across the width of the loom and tie it to the sides. Tape the warp sections to this stick.

10. Thread the loom as for warping back-to-front.

Note: The tubes on the spool rack are heavier at the beginning of the warping process. This weight makes the first sections tighter than later ones. It is best to have the tighter sections on the outside edges. *Do not start at one side and fill sections in order straight across the warp* as this will produce rugs with warps tight on one side and loose on the other. Likewise, starting at the center and working to the edges will produce rugs with rippled edges.

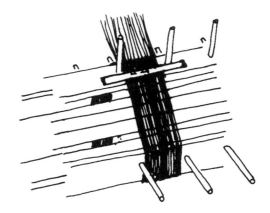

A-23. **Completed section** with cut warp ends taped and pinned into place.

Hints for Sectional Warping

• An easy way to count revolutions is to attach a cord to the beam and wrap the required number of revolutions in the opposite direction. Tie a nail to the end of the cord to act as a weight. As the warp is wound on, the cord will unwrap. Stop winding when the cord is completely unwound.

• Some looms are equipped with a threaded extension rod to the warp beam. A metal tab or nut is placed on the threads. The tab "walks" or moves along the threaded rod as the beam turns and falls off when the required number of turns have been completed. A trip counter attached to the loom is another way to count revolutions of the beam. However, it takes some ingenuity to attach this small metal box to the loom.

When I rewarp my loom and tie on a new warp
to the warp that is left in, I take a cup of warm
water and dip each section of knots. . . . The knots
will tighten as they dry and will not come undone
when they go through the heddles. [I have also read
that] women have trouble with the outside of the
rugs being wavy when they take them out. I pull the
outside warp of each rug to make the rags even with
the middle of the rug before [I] tie the warp in
knots. [I] do that from each end towards the middle
to make it even.

Mrs. Alice Magathan
The Shuttle, 1963

• To calculate warp length, measure the circumference of an empty section of the beam. Measure it again when filled. Add the two numbers and divide by 2 (average them), then multiply by the number of revolutions. This calculation takes into account the build-up of warp on the beam (i.e., as the section fills, each layer is longer than the previous one).

• Nearly all loom manufacturers make sectional beams. Dowels can be added to a plain wooden beam. For those without woodworking skills, wood strips with pegged sections are available.

Tying-on a Second Warp Using the Sectional Beam

When the warp has been completely woven, a second warp may be tied on. This eliminates re-threading of the shafts and reed. In the back of the loom, cut threads straight across and tie in loose knots behind the heddles. Remove remaining threads from the warp beam. Cut the threads in front of the loom about 12" from the reed. Put new warp on the warp beam. Tie the new warp ends to the ends of the old warp hanging from the heddles in the back. Use a weaver's knot, square knot, or overhand knot. Draw the new warp slowly through the heddles and the reed from the back to the front. Guide the knots through carefully. Cut behind the knots and tie the ends of the new warp to the front apron rod.

If a manual does not come with your loom, or if it has been lost, there are several sources for sectional warping information. The Loom Manual Library has reprints of loom instruction books. See *Suppliers List* for prices and addresses.

Selected Bibliography

Creager, Clara. *All About Weaving, A Comprehensive Guide to the Craft.* Garden City, New York: Doubleday & Company, Inc., 1984, pages 95–99.

Groff, Russell E. *Sectional Warping Made Easy.* Robin & Russ Handweavers (533 North Adams St., McMinnville, OR 97128)

Held, Shirley E. *Weaving, a Handbook for Fiber Craftsmen.* New York: Holt, Rinehart and Winston, Inc., 1973.

Appendix III

Health Hazards
of Rag Weaving

Here are some health problems faced by weavers who produce rag rugs on a limited production scale.

Cotton Lint and Dust

Breathing the lint from rags is perhaps the most serious hazard to rag rug weavers. Lint piles up in handfuls under the loom and settles on everything in sight. Because dust inhalation in cotton textile factories can cause brown lung, handweavers should also guard against that danger. Take these simple precautions.

• Always tear fabrics outdoors, preferably on a windy day.

• Vacuum the rag preparation and weaving area often.

• Wear a mask. The 3M mask 8710 protects against cotton lint and dust and is available at many hardware and paint stores. Read packages carefully because not all types of masks provide cotton dust protection.

Other Problems

Weaving is hard work and it can cause physical stress. Common sense will prevent some problems that plague weavers.

• It is always more comfortable to work in non-binding, loose clothing.

• Many steps in the warping and weaving process can cause back strain. When threading the loom, try to sit on a low stool at eye level to the heddles. During weaving, keep the loom bench high; many weavers stand to weave rugs. Some loom benches are slanted toward the loom. This is a very comfortable weaving position (no, you won't slide off!).

• Your feet and ankles may swell if you sit at the loom for long periods. Getting up and walking around periodically will alleviate this problem.

• "Weavers bottom" is caused by sitting on a hard loom bench, and is aggravated by the side-to-side motion of throwing the shuttle. A cushion covered in absorbent cotton fabric provides relief.

Glossary

Apron. A canvas cloth that fastens the apron bar to the warp or cloth beam.

Apron Bars. Sturdy bars or rods to which the warp is attached at the front and back of the loom.

Beam. *See* Breast Beam, Cloth Beam, Plain Beam, Sectional Beam, Warp Beam.

Beaming. Winding a warp onto the back beam of a loom.

Beater. The movable frame that holds the reed. Also called *batten*, *lathe*, and *lay*.

Brake. The device that maintains tension on the warp beam.

Breast Beam. Rigid beam at the front of the loom over which the woven cloth passes to the cloth beam below.

Carpet Warp. Heavy cotton yarn, usually 8/4, used for weaving rag rugs.

Castle. The central structure of the loom that supports the shafts.

Chain. Name given to the rope of warp as it comes from the warping device measured and counted. In some older manuals "chain" is synonymous with "warp".

Chaining. Putting loops in the warp as it is removed from the warping device to keep the threads from tangling.

Choke Ties. A series of tight ties made around the warp at the time of winding to ensure that the warp ends stay together until they are wound onto the loom.

Clove Hitch. A knot used to tie treadle, lamm, and shaft cords. Also called *snitch* and *loom knot*.

Cloth Beam. Rotating front beam of the loom on which the finished cloth is wound as it is woven.

Counterbalance Loom. A loom with a pulley system at the top that lowers threads when treadled. A sinking shed loom.

Cross. See Warp Cross.

Dent. The slots in the reed used for spacing warp ends.

Double Sley. Two warp threads put through each dent in the reed.

Draft. A drawing of a weave pattern on graph paper showing its threading and treadling order.

Draw-In. The pulling in or narrowing of the rug as it is woven caused by too much weft tension.

Dressing the Loom. Putting measured warp ends on the loom in an orderly fashion.

End. See Warp End.

Fell Line. The last row of weaving on the loom.

Filler. A few rows of heavy yarn woven into a new warp to spread it. Waste yarn or rags woven between pieces to reserve warp for fringe.

Filling. See Weft.

Fly-Shuttle. A shuttle propelled across the shuttle race either by the action of the beater or by a cord pulled by the weaver.

Harness. See Shaft.

Heading. A few rows of weaving at the beginning or end of a rug. Headings are often turned under for hems.

Heddle. A flat metal strip, string, or wire with an eye in its center through which a warp end is threaded.

Jack Loom. A loom on which the shafts rise when treadled. A rising shed loom.

Laid-In. Pattern achieved by inserting short fabric strips of contrasting color in the same shed on top of the last woven rag shot.

Lamms. Bars that connect the shafts to the treadles.

Lease Sticks. Flat, smooth, thin sticks inserted in the warp to preserve the warp cross.

Loom. A frame for holding the warp ends under tension and manipulating them for weaving.

Mill. See Reel.

Pawl. A catch lever of a ratchet. Sometimes called a *dog*.

Pick. See Shot.

Plain Beam. A warp beam not divided into sections. Used with chain warping methods.

Plain Weave. A weave in which the shuttle passes over and under the warp ends one by one as in darning. Also called *tabby*.

Raddle. A flat, narrow board with nails or pegs standing at one- or two-inch intervals. Used to spread the warp while it is being wound onto the back beam of the loom.

Ratchet. A wheel with notches or teeth used with a pawl or dog to put tension on the cloth and warp beams of the loom.

Reed. A metal, comb-like device placed in the beater to space warp ends evenly and drive the filling up against the woven fabric. Sometimes called *sley* or *comb*.

Reed Hook. A short, S-shaped hook used for drawing the warp ends through the dents of the reed. Also called *sley hook* and *draw-in hook*.

Reel. Large, barrel-like rotating frame around which long lengths of warp are wound.

Sectional Beam. A warp beam with pegs every two inches. Necessary for sectional warping.

Sectional Warping. Method by which the warp threads are wound directly from spools onto the sectional warp beam of a loom.

Selvedge. Edges of fabric formed by turning of wefts.

Sett. The number of warp ends per inch in the reed.

Shaft. A frame that holds a group of heddles on the loom.

Shed. The opening made in the warp in front of the reed through which the weft is passed.

Shot. A single passage of filling thread through the shed; a single throw of the shuttle. Also called *pick*.

Shuttle. Device that holds and carries the filling through the warp.

Shuttle Race. The bottom ledge of the beater on which the shuttle rides.

Single Sley. One warp thread put through each dent in the reed.

Sley. To thread the warp through the dents in the reed.

Sley Hook. See Reed Hook.

Spool Rack. An upright frame used to hold spools or cones of warp yarn for sectional warping.

Stretcher. See Temple.

Tabby. Plain weave in which the odd-numbered warp ends form one part of the shed and the even numbered form the other.

Take-Up. The amount of additional warp length used in the process of floating over and under the filler.

Temple. Adjustable wooden bar with protruding nails placed across the web during weaving to prevent selvedges from drawing in. Also called *stretcher*.

Tension Box. A device for maintaining tension on warp threads during sectional warping.

Threading Hook. A long-handled hook used for drawing warp ends through the eyes of the heddles.

Tie-Up. The prescribed manner in which the treadles are fastened to the lamms and/or the shafts.

Treadles. Pedals used to raise or lower the shafts on a loom.

Twill. A four-shaft weave in which the weft makes a diagonal pattern.

Warp. The lengthwise threads stretched on the loom.

Warp Beam. Rotating back beam on which unwoven warp is stored.

Warp Cross. The cross formed when warp ends are wound in a figure-eight. The warp cross facilitates the spreading and threading of the warp.

Warp End. An individual length of warp yarn.

Warp-Face. A weave in which the warp threads cover the weft.

Warping Board. A heavy, wooden frame with pegs upon which the warp ends are measured prior to beaming the warp.

Web. The fabric created by interlacing warp and weft.

Weft. The rags or yarns that are interwoven with the warp. Also called *filling* and *woof*.

Weft-Face. A weave in which the weft yarns cover the warp completely.

Suppliers List

The following list of sources is intended to help you find suitable warp yarns, rag wefts, loopers, and rag cutting tools. Many of these supplies are available at weaving shops.

Warps, Wefts, and Equipment

Eaton Yarns
P.O. Box 665
Tarrytown, NY 10591
(914) 631-1550 or (914) 946-9180

Edgemont Yarn Service, Inc.
P.O. Box 205
Washington, KY 41096
(800) 446-5977
edgemont@maysvilleky.net

The Ewe Tree, Inc.
61 Geoppert Rd.
Peninsula, OH 44264
(216) 650-6777

Glimåkra Looms 'n Yarns
1338 Ross St.
Petaluma, CA 94954-6502
(800) 289-9276

Great Northern Weaving
P.O. Box 462
Kalamazoo, MI 49004-0462
(800) 370-7235

Halcyon Yarn
12 School St.
Bath, ME 04530
(800) 341-0282
www.halcyonyarn.com

J. B. Company
742 Hanover Ave.
Allentown, PA 18103
(610) 435-5869

Leesburg Looms and Supply
201 N. Cherry St.
Van Wert, OH 45891
(800) 329-9254

WEBS
P.O. Box 147
Northampton, MA 01061-0147
(413) 584-2225
FAX (413) 584-1603

Yarn Barn of Kansas
930 Massachusetts
Lawrence, KS 66044
(800) 468-0035

Canadian Sources for Rag Rug Weavers

Camilla Valley Farm Weavers' Supply
P.O. Box 341
Orangeville, ON
L9W 2Z7
(519) 941-0736
www.CamillaValleyFarm.com

Maurice Brassard & Fils, Inc.
1573 Savoie, P.O. Box 4
Plessisville, PQ
G6L 2Y6
Phone (819) 362-2408

Nordic Studio
June Hanson
R.R. 2
Lunenburg, ON
K0C 1R0
Phone (613) 346-2373

Wefts

Braid-Aid
Rt. 53
Pembroke, MA 02359
(617) 826-6091

CJ's
2430 16th Dr.
Friendship, WI 53934
(608) 339-3849

Cherokee Byproducts
P.O. Box 3307
Spartenburg, SC 29304

Dorr Mill Store
P.O. Box 88
Guild, NH 03754-0088
(603) 863-1197

Flathead Industries
66 4th Ave. W.N.
Kalispell, MT 59903
(406) 755-7656

Modern Loopers
526 W. Lebanon St.
Mt. Airy, NC 27030
(910) 786-7780

Pendleton Woolen Mill Store
8550 S.E. McLoughlin Blvd.
Portland, OR 97222
(503) 273-2786

Rhino Rug Supply
1642 Plumtree Rd.
Fargo, ND 58102
(701) 280-1858

Riverbend Yarns
48 McHenry Dr. SW
Rome, GA 30161
(706) 236-9282

VT Rugs
P.O. Box 485
Johnson, VT 05656
(802) 635-2434 or (800) 639-1592

The Weaver's Knot
508 Inlet Dr.
Seneca, SC 29672
(800) 680-7747 orders

Consult the classified ads of current weaving magazines for additional suppliers.

Equipment

Fabric Cutters

The Harry M. Fraser Company
R&R Machine Company
433 Duggins Rd.
Stoneville, NC 27048
(336) 573-9830

Mask

3M Company Mask
Stock #8710 or #8560/8710
Available from industrial supply companies and som paint stores. The mask should be worn when cutting tearing, and weaving with rags.

Eastman Machine Company
779 Washington St.
Buffalo, NY 14203-1396
(716) 856-2200

Flathead Industries
66 4th Ave. W.N.
Kalispell, MT 59903
(406) 755-7656

Additional Sources for Rags

IN-WEAVE
823 Central Ave.
Hawarden, IA 51023
(800) 646-9328
inweave@inweave.com
www.inweave.com

Princeton Weaving and Fabric Shoppe
Deanna Brown
34301 Puma St. NW
Princeton, MN 55371
(763) 389-4156
deeweave@sherbtel.net

To find mills and factories for rags in your area, look in *Davison's Textile Blue Book* or the *Thomas Register* at the public library.

Selvedges and Remnants

Pendleton
The Woolen Mill Store
8550 S. E. McLoughlin Blvd.
Portland, OR 97222
(503) 535-5786

Books

The Unicorn
1338 Ross Street
Petaluma, CA 94954-6502
(800) 289-9276

Instruction Manuals for Factory-Built Looms

The Loom Manual Library, Historic Looms
    of America
c/o Janet Meany
5672 North Shore Drive
Duluth, MN 55804
(218) 525-5778

A part of Historic Looms of America, The Loom Manual Library has instructions for many factory-built looms, old and new, including complete instructions for sectionally warping the Studio Loom and the Weaver's Delight Loom (The Newcomb Loom Co., Davenport, IA) with the "Anderson" and "Hollywood" weaves.

Historic Looms of America
(Formerly The Newcomb Looms Historical
    Society)
c/o Theresa Lee Trebon
10619 Sterling Rd.
Sedro Wooley, WA 98284
(360) 856-6532

Rag Rug Newsletter

The Weaver's Friend
(published twice yearly)
c/o Janet Meany
5672 North Shore Drive
Duluth, MN 55804
(218) 525-5778

The objective of this biannual newsletter is to serve the interests and concerns of rag rug weavers, to promote an appreciation of the history of rag rug weaving, and to explore contemporary applications of the craft. Send your name and address to the above address for a free introductory copy.

Bibliography

Rag Rug References

Allen, Heather L. *Weaving Contemporary Rag Rugs*. Asheville, NC: Lark Books, 1998.

Atwater, Mary M. *Handwoven Rugs*. Coupeville, WA: HTH Publishers, 1948. Shuttle Craft Guild Monograph 29.

———. *The Shuttlecraft Book of American Handweaving*. Coupeville, WA: HTH Publishers, 1987.

Baizerman, Suzanne and Karen Searle. *Finishes in the Ethnic Tradition*. St. Paul, MN: Dos Tejedoras, 1978.

Barrett, Clotilde. "Weaving in Quebec." *The Weaver's Journal*, 6, 4, (Spring 1982), 8–11.

Bateman, Wendy E. "Bring Me Your Shirts, Your Sweaters, and Pants." *Handwoven*, 14, 5 (Nov/Dec 1993), 54.

Benedict, Alma Taylor. "Country Charm Rugs." *Handwoven*, 17, 1 (Jan/Feb 1996), 69–71.

Bradley, Louise. "Rag Placemat." *Handwoven*, 20, 4 (Sep/Oct 1999), 43–44, 73–74.

Broden, Marta and Gertrud Ingers. *Trasmattor Och Andra Mator*. Stockholm: LTs förlag, 1966.

"Clasped Weft." *Handwoven*, 7, 4 (Sep/Oct 1986), 58–59.

Collingwood, Peter. *Rug Weaving Techniques: Beyond the Basics*. Loveland, CO: Interweave Press, 1990.

———. *The Techniques of Rug Weaving*. New York, NY: Watson Guptill, 1968.

"Coordinating Rags." *Handwoven*, 12, 1 (Jan/Feb 1991), 60–62.

Cripps, Alice K. *Adventures in Weaving on a 2 Harness Loom*. Maysville, KY: January & Wood Company, Inc., 1950.

Erickson, Johanna. "A Feast of Colors for Production Rag Weaving." *Handwoven*, 14, 5 (Nov/Dec 1993), 56–57.

———. "A Summer Home." *Handwoven*, 10, 3 (May/June 1989), 46.

———. "Log Cabin Rag Rugs." *Shuttle, Spindle & Dyepot*, 20, 3 (Summer, 1989), 22–25.

———. "Rag Rugs Not Always Made From Rags." *Threads*, 1, 3 (Feb/Mar 1986), 40–41.

———. *Rag Weaving Gimmicks and Tricks*. Self Published: 48 Chester St., Watertown, MA 02472, 1999. (New, Revised Illustrated Edition.)

———. "Ragtime." *Shuttle, Spindle & Dyepot*, 14, 3, (Summer 1983), 41–45.

Evans, Jane A. *A Joy Forever*. St. Paul, MN: Dos Tejedoras, 1991.

——— and Kay Reiber. "Patchwork Rugs." *Weaver's*, 22 (3rd Quarter, 1993), 12–14.

———. "Pictorial Rugs on Four Shafts." *Handwoven*, 14, 5 (Nov/Dec 1993), 58–61.

———. "Picture Perfect." *Weaver's*, 12 (1st Quarter 1991), 22–25.

———. "Pigments of the Imagination." *Weaver's*, 23 (4th Quarter 1993), 24–25.

———. "Polychrome Rugs." *Weaver's*, 9 (2nd Quarter 1990), 36–40.

———. "Rags To Roses: A Weaver's Garden." *Weaver's*, 11 (4th Quarter 1990), 48–51.

———. "Rags Unlimited." *Handwoven*, 2, 3 (May 1981), 44.

———. "The Thick and Thin of Shadow Weave." *Handwoven*, 11, 2 (Mar/Apr 1990), 40–42.

———. "Warp Stuffer Weave with Shaft Switching Applications." *Handwoven*, 4, 3 (May/June 1983), 72–73.

Finch, Joan Freitag. "Rags at Work." *Shuttle, Spindle & Dyepot*, 6, 4 (Fall 1985), 72–75.

Fredlund, Jane and Birgit Wiberg. *Rag Rug Weaves: Patterns from Sweden*. Stockholm: LTs förlag, 1986.

From Rags to. . . . Edited by HGA Publications Committee. West Hartford, CT: Handweavers Guild of America, 1982. Baker's Dozen Series.

"Glad Rags." *Handwoven*, 18, 3 (May/June 1997), 40–41.

Gordon, Beverly. "Rag Rugs, Part II: The Shaker Technique." *Shuttle, Spindle & Dyepot*, 8, 1 (Winter 1976), 83–85.

———. *Shaker Textile Arts*. Hanover, MA: University Press of New England, 1980.

Hamstead, Janet. "Golden Glow Vest Fabric." *Handwoven*, 16, 5 (Nov/Dec 1995), 55.

Harter, Joyce. "Double Warp Overlay for Rugs." *Handwoven*, 14, 5 (Nov/Dec 1993), 64–66.

Harvey, Nancy. "Double Corduroy Shag Rug." *Weaver's*, 7, 2 (Winter 1994), 18, 19.

Hillenburg, Nancy. "Shaker Textiles." *The Weaver's Journal*, 8, 1 (Spring 1983), 22–24.

Hinchcliff, John and Angela Jeffs. *Rugs from Rags*. London: Orbis Publishing, 1977.

Höykinpuro, Anja. "How to Use a Temple." *Handwoven*, 15, 4 (Sep/Oct 1994), 48–49.

———. "Ikat for Rag Rug Weavers." *Handwoven*, 15, 5 (Nov/Dec 1994), 54–57.

———. "Rag Rug Weaving." *Weaver's*, Issue 16 (1st Quarter, 1992), 18–21.

———. "Weaving with Poppana." *Handwoven*, 18, 3 (May/June 1997), 38–39.

"If You have Four Harnesses." *Handweaver & Craftsman*, 24, 4 (July/Aug 1973), 39.

Irwin, Bobbie. "Danish Twined Rag Rugs." *The Weaver's Journal*, 10, 4 (Spring 1986), 32–36.

———. *Twined Rag Rugs*. Iola, WI: Krause Publications, 2000.

"Johanna Erickson's Art is the Fabric of Everyday Life." *Handwoven*, 26, 2 (Mar/Apr 1995), 56–57.

Johansson, Lillemor, Pia Wedderien and Marie Rolander, eds. *Swedish Rag Rugs: 35 New Designs*. Glimåkra, Sweden: FörlagsAB Vävhästen, 1995.

Johnson, Geraldine Niva. *Weaving Rag Rugs: A Women's Craft in Western Maryland*. Knoxville, TN: The University of Tennessee Press, 1985.

Johnston, Coleen L. "Rag Rug Revisited." *Handwoven*, 12, 4 (Sep/Oct 1994), 50.

———. "Start With a Room-Sized Rug—And Work Up." *Handwoven*, 8, 4 (Sep/Oct 1987), 85–87.

Kaplan, Donna. "The Potential of Poppana." *Shuttle Spindle & Dyepot*, 18, 3 (Summer 1997), 27–30.

Krook, Inga. "From Rags to Riches." *Handwoven*, 4, 3 (Summer 1983), 32–38.

———. "'Maria' Rag Rug." *Handwoven*, 6, 3 (Summer 1985), 1–14, 56–57.

Leinonen, Virpi. *Kaunista Kangaspuilla*. Helsingissä: Kustannusosakeyhtiö Otava, 1981.

Lewes, Klares and Helen Hutton. *Rug Weaving*. New York, NY: Charles T. Branford Company, 1962.

———. *Your Rugmaking*. Peoria, IL: Sylvan Press, 1949.

Ligon, Linda C., ed. *A Rug Weaver's Source Book*. Loveland, Colorado: Interweave Press, Inc., 1984.

———. "Sheepskate Weaving." *Handwoven*, 5, 4 (Sep/Oct 1984), 70.

Linden, Deborah. "Shadow Rags." *Weaver's*, 4, 4, (1st Quarter, 1992), 37.

Linder, Olive. "Pushing the Limits with Rags." *Handwoven*, 2, 3 (May 1991), 51–53.

Little, Frances. *Early American Textiles*. New York, NY: Century Company, 1931.

Lochner, Arnold. "So, You'd Like to Build a Rug." *Handwoven*, 17, 1 (Jan/Feb 1996), 66–68.

Loud, Dana. "From Rags to Riches: Artful Recycling." *Fiberarts*, 13, 5 (Sep/Oct 1986), 23.

Madden, Gail. "Country Skys Runner." *Handwoven*, 17, 1 (Jan/Feb 1996), 65, 86.

Mattila, Wynne. "Game Plan for Rugs." *Handwoven*, 18, 1 (Jan/Feb 1997), 58.

Mattor: Med Randor och Rutor. Helsingborg, Sweden: AB Boktryck, 1980.

Meany, Janet K. "Log Cabin Rag Rugs." *The Weaver's Journal*, 9, 4 (Spring 1985), 50–55.

———. "Rag Rug Traditions." *The Weaver's Journal*, 9, 4 (Spring 1985), 56–58.

Nordin, Eva-Lisa. *Trasmattor: 44 modeller i farg*. Vasteros, Sweden: ICA Bokförlag, 1981.

Nye, Thelma M. *Swedish Weaving*. New York, NY: Van Nostrand Reinhold, 1969.

Nylén, Anna-Maja. "Rag Weaving: a History of Necessity." An excerpt from *Swedish Handcraft* in *Handwoven*, 8, 33 (May/June 1987), 38.

Oldenburg, Betty. "Stenciled Rag Rug." *Handwoven*, 5, 3 (Summer 1984), 74.

Oles, Jery. "Mystery Sun Rug." *The Weaver's Journal*, 7, 4 (Spring 1984), 10–11.

Patrick, Jane, ed. *Just Rags*. Handwoven's Design Collection 8. Loveland, CO: Interweave Press, Inc., 1985.

Pfaff, Paula. "Sock Top Bathmat." *The Weaver's Journal*, 10, 4 (Spring 1986), 49.

Plath, Iona. *The Craft of Handweaving*. New York, NY: Charles Scribner's Sons, 1972.

"Rag Rugs." *Handwoven*, 18, 4 (Sep/Oct 1997), 34–41.

"Rag Rugs." *The Weaver's Journal*, 4, 1 (July 1979), 22–24.

"Rags." *Handwoven*, 2, 3 (May 1981), 43–53.

"Rags to Riches." *The Weaver's Journal*, 6, 3 (Winter 1981–1982), 30–32.

"Rag Weavers' Tips for Wonderful Wearable Clothing." *Handwoven*, 16, 2 (Mar/Apr 1995), 48–57.

"Ragtime Vests: Pushing the Limits." *Handwoven*, 10, 5 (Nov/Dec 1989), 46–47.

"Recycled Weaving." *Handwoven*, 12, 4 (Sep/Oct 1991), 46–51.

"Recycling—Ragtime!" *Interweave*, 5, 2 (Summer 1978), 22–23.

Roberts, Diana. "Rag Prep." *Handwoven*, 2, 3 (May 1981), 53.

Roberts, Trudie. "Rag Fashion." *Threads*, 28 (Apr/May 1990), 48–51.

Rogers, Carrie M. "The Story of My Dining Room Rug." *The Weaver's Journal*, 6, 4 (Spring 1982), 26–27.

Rossetter, Tabitha Wilson. "The Acadian Textile Heritage." *Fiberarts*, 8, 3 (May/June 1981), 29–32.

"Rugs." *Weaver's*, Issue 42 (Winter 1998), 11–39.

Ruyak, Jacqueline. "Miyoshi Shirahata, Weaver of Hemp and Rags." *Handwoven*, 16, 1 (Jan/Feb 1995), 77–80.

Saulson, Sarah F. "California Rags." *Shuttle, Spindle & Dyepot*, 18, 1 (Winter 1986), 43–48.

Scorgie, Jean. "Cotton Rag Rug." *Handwoven*, 12, 5 (Nov/Dec 1991), 61, 90.

———. "Poppana Tapestry Jacket." *Handwoven*, 4, 3 (May/June 1983), 48, 84.

Selander, Malin. *Weave a Weave*. Stockholm: LTs förlag, 1986.

Sharpee, Debra K., "Diamond Rugs." *Weaver's*, Issue 29 (Fall 1995), 42–43.

———. " 'Color Bars' Rug," *Weaver's*, Issue 35 (Spring 1997), 26–27.

Snover, Susan. "Rag Rugs on Overshot." *The Weaver's Journal*, 5, 4 (Spring 1981), 22–23.

Stoehr, Mary Kay. "Weave a Special Place." *Handwoven*, 5, 2 (Mar/Apr 1984), 50–51.

Tallarovic, Joanne. "The New Rippsmatta." *Shuttle, Spindle & Dyepot*, 19, 2 (Spring, 1988), 36–42.

Talley, Charles. "Portraits of Three Weavers: Marja Graset Andersson." *Fiberarts*, 8, 2 (Mar/Apr 1981), 48–49.

Tidball, Harriet. *The Weaver's Book*. New York, NY: Collier Books, 1976.

———. *Two Harness Textiles: The Two Harness Weaves*. Coupeville, WA: HTH Publishers, 1967. Shuttle Craft Guild Monograph 20.

Tod, Osma Gallinger. *The Joy of Handweaving*. New York, NY: Bonanza Books, 1964.

Tod, Osma Gallinger and Josephine Couch Del Deo. *Designing and Making Handwoven Rugs*. New York, NY: Dover Publications, 1976.

"Trudie Roberts' Rag Weave Sweatshirts." *Handwoven*, 10, 3 (May/June 1989), 60–62.

"Unusual Rag Wefts." *Handwoven*, 15, 5 (Nov/Dec 1994), 60–61.

Waggoner, Phyllis, "Double Corduroy Rug." *The Weaver's Journal*, 9, 2 (Fall 1986), 42–47.

———. "Two Block Rug in Bound Weave." *The Weaver's Journal*, 12, 1 (Summer 1987), 26–31.

"Weaving with Rags." *Handwoven*, 2, 3 (May 1981), 80.

White, Ruth. "Rag Rugs with Overlapping Weft Ends." *The Weaver's Journal*, 6, 4 (Spring 1982), 28.

Wiley, Elizabeth. "Ripsmatta." *Handwoven*, 20, 3 (May/June 1999), 48–51.

Woelfle, Gretchen. "An American Heritage: Three Rug Making Traditions: Rag Rugs." *Fiberarts*, 7, 5 (Sep/Oct 1980), 31–33.

"Wonderful Rugs." *Handwoven*, 14, 5 (Nov/Dec 1993), 53–66.

Wroten, Barbara. "Glad Rags." *Shuttle, Spindle & Dyepot*,

15, 4 (Fall 1984), 28–29.

Yamamoto, Judith. "A Room-Size Rag Rug." *Handwoven*, 12, 4 (Sep/Oct 1994), 48–49, 75.

Yoshida, Shin-Ichiro and Dai Williams. *Riches from Rags: Saki-ori & Other Recycling Traditions in Japanese Rural Clothing*. San Francisco Craft & Folk Art Museum, Exhibition Catalogue, May 28 to August 6, 1994.

Loom References

Look to these sources for photographs and drawings of looms. Starred entries are especially recommended for handmade looms.

Adrosko, Rita. "American Coverlet Looms." In Shaeffer, Margaret. *Made in New York State: Handwoven Coverlets 1820–1860: A Traveling Exhibition*. Watertown, NY: Jefferson County Historical Society, 1985.

*Adrosko, Rita. *Plans for Making a 19th Century American Loom*. St. Paul, MN: Dos Tejedoras Fiber Arts Publications, 1992. Originally published by the Smithsonian Institution, Washington D.C., 1968. Available from Interweave Press.

Benson, Anna and Neil Warburton. *Looms and Weaving*. Aylesbury, Bucks, U.K.: Shire Publications, 1986. Shire Album 154.

Bogdonoff, Nancy Dick. *Handwoven Textiles of Early New England*. Harrisburg, PA: Stackpole Books, 1975.

Broudy, Eric. *The Book of Looms*. New York, NY: Van Nostrand Reinhold, 1979. Reissued in paperback edition in 1993.

Burnham, Dorothy K. and Harold B. *Keep Me Warm One Night: Early Handweaving in Eastern Canada*. Toronto, Canada: University of Toronto Press, 1972.

Channing, Marion L. *The Textile Tools of Colonial Homes*. Marion, MA: Reynolds-DeWalt, 1969.

Colwell, Ken. "Looms from the Past." *Handwoven*, 2, 3 (May 1981), 34–37.

*Creager, Clara. *All About Weaving, A Comprehensive Guide to the Craft*. Garden City, NY: Doubleday, 1984. Chapter 1 is a survey of loom types.

Cyrus-Zetterström, Ulla. *Manual of Swedish Weaving*. Stockholm: LTs förlag, 1984.

"Fiberarts Equipment Directory." *Fiberarts*, 6, 1 (Jan/Feb 1979), 27–74.

Fisher, Leonard Everett. *The Weavers*. New York, NY: Franklin Watts, 1966. (illustration)

Grenander Nyberg, Gertrud. *Lanthemmens vävstolar*. Nordiska museets Handlingar 84. Stockholm, Sweden: Goteborgs offsettryckeri AB, 1975.

Halvorsen, Caroline. *Håndbok I Vevning*. Oslo: J. W. Cappelens Förlag, 1934.

"The Hands That Make Your Looms." *Handwoven*, 2, 3 (May 1981), 25–30.

Hausner, Walter. "Handlooms in Use Today." *Handweaver & Craftsman*, (Fall 1964), 22–23, 40.

Hooper, Luther. *Hand-Loom Weaving: Plain and Ornamental*. London, England: Pitman, 1920. New York, NY: Taplinger, 1979.

Keasbey, Doramay. "In the Beginning: Choosing a Floor Loom: Sinking Vs. Rising Shed." *Interweave*, 5, 3 (Summer 1980), 50–53.

Little, Frances. *Early American Textiles*. New York, NY: Century, 1931.

Meany, Janet K. "Looms in the 1920s to 1960s: An Overview." *Handwoven*, 11, 3 (May/June 1990), 66, 86.

*Osterkamp, Peggy. *Peggy Osterkamp's New Guide to Weaving, Number 1, How to Wind a Warp and Use a Paddle*, 1992. Number 2, *Warping Your Loom & Tying on New Warps*, 1995.
Sausalito, CA 94965: Lease Sticks Press.

Ross, Nan. "Those Musty Old Looms." *Shuttle, Spindle & Dyepot*, 8, 2 (Spring 1977), 43, 44.

Saylor, Mary C. "A Reflection of the Past." *Shuttle, Spindle & Dyepot*, 7, 3 (Summer 1976), 26–28.

Straub, Marianne. *Hand Weaving and Cloth Design*. New York, NY: Viking, 1977.

Tovey, John. *The Technique of Weaving*. New York, NY: Scribner, 1965.

Trebon, Theresa Lee. "Handweaving in the Industrial Age: 1865–1920." *Handwoven*, 14, 3 (May/June 1993), 49–51.

———. "The Newcomb Looms Historical Society." *Shuttle, Spindle & Dyepot*, 20, 3 (Summer 1989), 76–80.

Wigginton, Elliot, ed. *Foxfire 2*. Garden City, NY: Anchor (Doubleday), 1973.

*Worst, Edward F. *Weaving with Foot Power Looms*. Milwaukee, WI: Bruce, 1918. New York, NY: Dover, 1974 (paperback).

Index

About the Authors

Janet Meany of Duluth, Minnesota, became interested in rag rugs in 1976 while doing a research project on weavers and their looms in the Two Harbors area of Minnesota during the U.S. Bicentennial celebration. She has organized a Minnesota loom documentation project, involving photographing antique looms throughout the state and interviewing their owners. Her articles on rag rugs and antique looms have appeared in *The Weaver's Journal; Shuttle, Spindle & Dyepot;* and *Handwoven* magazines. Janet is a founder of the Minnesota Federation of Weavers and Fiber Artists, and has served as Minnesota state representative for the Handweavers Guild of America. She has taught weaving classes at the University of Minnesota, Duluth, and classes and workshops on rag rugs throughout the Midwest and at weaver's conferences.

Paula Pfaff is a Saint Paul, Minnesota, production weaver specializing in custom and production rag rug weaving, clothing, and interior or furnishing fabrics. She grew up in a small Minnesota town where rag rugs were an important part of her family's household decor. The art of weaving merges her love of fiber, fabric, and color. She enjoys carrying on the rag rug weaving tradition and exploring rag rug lore. As a commission weaver, she has woven rag carpeting for restored historic buildings, including the Minnesota Governor's mansion in Saint Paul, and the McKay farmhouse in Hudson, Wisconsin. Paula has taught classes and workshops on rag rug weaving at the University of Minnesota's Summer Arts Program, the Weaver's Guild of Minnesota's weaving school, and at weaver's conferences.